Review

Global Gypsies have nailed it with "How to be an Award-Winning Tour Guide"! It's comprehensive, entertaining, and full of great advice.

Ryan Mossny
Two Feet and a Heartbeat Tours

'The book is an excellent practical introduction to the world of tour guiding. Written by two acknowledged leaders in the field, it is a must read for anyone interested in becoming a guide. It also is a great resource for established tour guides who are seeking to learn more about their profession and how to become an even better guide. It covers all aspects of tour guiding in an easy-to-follow practical format supported by photos taken on their own tours. I commend the book and recommend it with confidence.'

Professor Ross K. Dowling OAM Ph.D. GAICD
Associate Head, School of Business
Edith Cowan University

'The most practical tour-guide training manual we've ever read and implemented. We'll be recommending it to all our industry colleagues!'

Graeme and Toni Dearle
Pemberton Discovery Tours

'This book will be a welcome addition to the training resources available for tour guides and other tourism professionals not only in Western Australia, but in other regions of Australia and around the world. I highly recommend it to anyone keen to get involved in our burgeoning tourism industry.'

Evan Hall
CEO, Tourism Council Western Australia

'I attended a Global Gypsies Tour-Guide Training Course about ten years ago. It was fantastic and provided me with an excellent springboard to achieving my hopes of becoming an outback tour guide. Since then, I've spent many happy and very rewarding years working as a freelance guide in some of the more remote areas of Western Australia. For those contemplating a career as a tour guide, this book is the next best thing to attending the training course. I regard it as recommended reading for anyone involved in the tourism industry.'

Terry Brewin
Freelance Tour Guide

'If you're thinking about becoming a guide, just started working in the industry, or are a guide with many years' experience, this book will make an excellent reference or timely reminder for all. Don't just buy it – use it!'

Tom Grove
Managing Director
Coates Wildlife Tours

How to Be an Award-Winning Tour Guide

Jeremy Perks & Jan Barrie

Library of Congress Control Number: 2015918161
ISBN: Hardcover   978-1-5144-4247-0
                 Softcover   978-1-5144-4246-3
                 eBook   978-1-5144-4245-6

Print information available on the last page.

Rev. date: 03/02/2016

To order additional copies of this book, contact:
Xlibris
1-800-455-039
www.Xlibris.com.au
Orders@Xlibris.com.au
707363

Contents

Foreword

By Associate Professor Jim Macbeth, B.Com, MA, Ph.D., Emeritus, Former Head of Tourism at Murdoch University, Western Australia

Two strangers came to see me at my Murdoch University office a few years after we had started the tourism course. It was 2001, and Jeremy Perks and Jan Barrie were running an outback tour company called Global Gypsies.

They were concerned about the lack of practical training for tour guides in Western Australia and wanted to share their experience in tour design and tour-guide training with others. They were keen to develop a short, hands-on training course for potential guides.

We talked about ecotourism, nature-based tourism, and outback travel. They said they wanted to contribute something to the tourism industry that is always necessary – skilled, knowledgeable, and ethical nature-based tour-guide training.

They asked if Murdoch University would like to become a partner in the new training course and suggested a plan by which we would offer them a venue for the classroom component and assist with some of the course content.

As designer of the social-science-based tourism course, I was keen for us to have strong links with the tourism industry and to be able to provide not only academic education for tourism students, but also contribute to the face-to-face tourism practitioner, something we couldn't do directly at that stage.

Coincidentally, I had a research interest in outback travel and, in subsequent years, was part of the Desert Knowledge Cooperative Research Centre. Jeremy and Jan had come to a person who shared their philosophy of outback travel, and the partnership began.

I've always been pleased that I went with my hunch in 2001 and facilitated the relationship between Global Gypsies and Murdoch University. As a result, dozens of potential guides have attended their tour-guide training courses, and Jeremy and Jan have now published this book. I believe they have made a valuable contribution to tour guiding in Western Australia through their continued efforts to 'raise the bar'. I wish them every success with *How to be an Award-Winning Tour Guide* and just wish I could go on all their tours!

Acknowledgements

We'd like to dedicate this book to our friend and industry colleague, Jeff Baylden (1952–2014) who, while employed by Pilbara TAFE in Karratha as a tourism lecturer, helped us to gain accreditation for our tour-guide training course, assisted with course content, undertook student assessment, and provided ongoing inspiration to us and to his many fortunate students, workmates, and fellow educators.

We'd also like to thank the following people who have provided the assistance, support, and encouragement over the years that has made this book possible:

- Associate Professor Jim Macbeth, B.Com, MA, Ph.D., Emeritus, who, while in charge of tourism at Murdoch University, sponsored our inaugural tour-guide training course.
- Anthea Kilminster, who, when employed as the CEO of the WA Hospitality and Tourism Industry Training Council, helped us gain funding and accreditation for the course.
- Cherie Toovey, professional tour guide, tourism lecturer, president of Tour Guides, WA, and former FACET Tour Guide of the Year, who helped write the content of the workbook for our tour-guide training course, continues to co-facilitate the sessions and made invaluable suggestions to the drafts of the book.
- The tour operators who have sent their staff on the course.
- The many individual students who have attended the course.

- Our enthusiastic and invaluable Global Gypsies team which has included Pam Vassi, Di Gardiner, Peter Sommer, Wally Harding, Ingo Helbig, Rebina Criddle, Jo Clews, Greg and Choccy Thomson, Richard Nicholls, Trevor Cocks (deceased), Eddy Tamlin, Geoff Couper, and more.

- Our sponsors, suppliers, and joint venture partners, including Adventure Wild, ARB 4×4 Accessories, Autospark Auto Electricians, Bam Creative, Coates Wildlife Tours, Coromal Caravans, Department of Parks & Wildlife Services, George Day Caravans, Muntz & Partners Accountants, Murdoch University, RAC Travel (WA), Robson Brothers 4WD Service & Repair, Tourism Council WA, Tourism Western Australia, Wandering Star Trailers, Western Travel Bug and many more.

- Geoff & Gillian Longworth, formerly owners of All Terrain Safaris, and their 1998 tour-guiding team for sharing their knowledge and friendship.

- The journalists and media outlets who have been so generous with their coverage, particularly Stephen Scourfield, travel editor, and his team at *West Australian Newspapers*.

- Our publisher, Xlibris, for their guidance, proofreading, and editorial suggestions.

- The hundreds of Global Gypsies clients who have participated in our tours and training courses since we established the company in 1997. Their loyalty, feedback, and support have been the source of much empirical content for this book, provided unforgettable memories and shared experiences, created lasting friendships, and motivated and inspired us to keep going for gold.

1

Your Tour Changed My Life!

Splash! Silvery fins broke through the water as the dolphins frolicked in the turquoise shallows. Their sleek bodies glistened in the sun as they dived and resurfaced. Three adult females and a calf broke away from the pod and headed for the white strip of beach where a large crowd of tourists stood watching excitedly.

We were leading a tour to a coastal community about 800 km north of Perth called Monkey Mia. It's a famous eco-destination on the shores of the Indian Ocean where animal lovers go to feed dolphins in the wild. Jeremy was the tour guide.

One of his clients, a tough, solidly built, retired English policeman, stood knee-deep in the lapping waves with his back to the crowd. He couldn't believe his luck! He'd been chosen by the park ranger to help feed the dolphins!

Conservative and reserved, this aging, hard-as-nails policeman had years of experience on the beat in London's back streets. He'd travelled all the way to Australia for one reason and one reason only – to see wild dolphins.

He took a fish from the plastic bucket and waved it in the water to tempt the approaching dolphins. One came close and softly tugged it from his hand. A second dolphin gave a squeaky greeting and grabbed the next fish. Cautiously, the protective mother swam over with her tiny calf. She bumped playfully against the man's legs with her slippery, sandpapery skin.

Both mother and baby nuzzled his hand; then, each took a fish. They circled him for several minutes, touching him gently, staying longer than usual. Then they turned, swam back out to sea, and rejoined the pod.

The tourists on the beach began to disperse, but the client didn't move. He stood statue-still, facing the horizon, transfixed. After several minutes, Jeremy waded out to check on him. The rough, gruff policeman was sobbing; tears were cascading down his cheeks. He was too overwhelmed and emotionally charged to move.

Jeremy stayed with him for a while. Eventually, when he regained his composure, the policeman said, 'This was the best experience of my life. It's changed me forever. How can I possibly thank you?'

Monkey Mia in Western Australia is a popular destination to interact with wild dolphins under the supervision of a park ranger. (Photo courtesy Global Gypsies.)

For this international visitor, it was a dream come true. He thought he'd been chosen at random; he never knew what had gone on behind the scenes to make the wildlife encounter possible. But we'd like to share it with you.

Dozens of people visit Monkey Mia each day to watch the feeding of the dolphins. Usually, several of the gregarious creatures come in to take fish from the ranger's hands. The ranger chooses only one lucky person from the crowd to assist with the task.

Jeremy knew this; he also knew that his client had little or no chance of being selected from the masses without a little help. Fortunately, he knew the ranger well and took him aside the day before.

'Mate, could you do me a huge favour? Could you possibly choose my client to be your dolphin feeder tomorrow? It would mean so much to him. I'll put him in a bright-red hat so you can find him.'

The next morning, the beach was crowded with tourists all hoping to be selected to help feed the dolphins. The ranger asked for an assistant; a hundred hands flew skywards. Spotting the man in the red hat, the ranger beckoned the policeman to come forward. The favour had a lasting impact.

As a tour guide, you have the power to touch somebody's life and to give them memories that will last forever. Only a handful of jobs can deliver such huge emotional rewards.

People often ask us why we're in this business. Obviously, we have a passion for travel, and we genuinely enjoy working with people. But one of the main reasons we love having a tour business is magic moments like these – those precious experiences that make you all misty and get your heart beating a little faster, those rare times when you feel you've made a real difference and have changed someone's life.

2

What is a Tour Guide?

If there was a television commercial about becoming a tour guide, it might go something like this . . .

Bored with your job? Love travel? Like working with people?
Then add some excitement to your life and become a tour guide!

Sounds like everybody's dream job, right? Well, yes and no. To help you decide if tour guiding is for you, we're going to take a closer look at the profession and highlight the pros and cons. Then if you do decide to give it a go (or want to improve your existing skills if you're already working as a guide), this book can help you become not just a tour guide, but an *award-winning tour guide*. So sit back and enjoy the ride; we're going to take you on the tour of your life!

But first, let's start at the beginning. What exactly *is* a tour guide and what does a guide actually do? Here's our definition:

A tour guide is an enthusiastic, knowledgeable,
responsible, passionate, multi-skilled
interpreter delivering a consistently high-quality visitor experience.

Here's our explanation of a tour guide's role:

To equip clients with the skills and knowledge to appreciate, respect, understand, and interact with natural, cultural, historical, or built attractions.

That's possibly a bit more complex than you thought – it's not just showing tourists around a venue or driving them from A to B, is it?

To us, tour guiding is one of the most exciting and personally rewarding careers you can pursue. It enables you to travel, learn about our wonderful world, share your knowledge and enthusiasm with others, and interact with a wide range of people. Best of all, it gives you the opportunity to deliver life-changing experiences to your clients. And that really *does* happen! When it does, it's the biggest buzz of all.

It's been said that if you find a job you love, you'll never work a day in your life. Well, that's certainly true of tour guiding; at least, that's been the case for us.

Guiding plays a critical role in the tourism industry – a good guide can often make or break a tour. Think for a moment about the best tour guide you've ever encountered. Apart from the activity itself, what made that tour so special? The information the guide imparted? The way the narrative was delivered? The guide's knowledge? Sense of humour? The personality that shone through behind the narrative? Or was it a combination of all these things?

Being a guide isn't easy, although it might appear so at first glance. A good tour guide needs to be a teacher, psychologist, actor, storyteller, even a shepherd – try getting a disparate group of human beings to follow you around for hours or even days while holding their interest and telling them a story! It's like herding cats!

In many countries (Borneo, Botswana, China, Kenya, Peru, New Zealand, South Africa, and the USA, for example), tour guiding is considered an honourable, highly esteemed, and enviable profession, a true calling and a highly respected long-term career. To become a tour guide in those places, you need licenses, accreditation, often a university degree, and a significant amount of training before you can proudly pin on a badge or don a uniform.

Yet in other parts of the world, regulation is minimal – our base of Western Australia (or WA as it's called) is one example. Consequently, for many people in WA, tour guiding is just a way of earning some extra cash between 'real' jobs, and the career doesn't enjoy the prestige or good reputation it has elsewhere. In spite of this, there are numerous highly professional tour companies and hundreds of fabulous tour guides here, not to mention the fantastic sights and experiences.

Yet we believe that more training and individual accreditation should be required in our state before tour guides are given the responsibility of running tours. This would help bring the profession up to the standards set by many other places, give guiding more credibility as a career, and raise the bar of individual guides by encouraging them to always strive for excellence.

The lack of individual regulation and the absence of practical, hands-on training was the main reason we developed our unique, short, hands-on tour-guide training course over a decade ago. The content of that course forms the basis of this book. We hope you enjoy it and find it beneficial.

Tour Guide Tale #1: Skip the Sarcasm

We like a joke and a touch of sarcasm as much as the next person, but using sarcasm in your tour-guide narrative is not a good idea. Some clients won't get the joke, while others (particularly overseas travellers who may have a different sense of humour and for whom English is a second language) may take what you say as fact!

A tour-guide mate of ours has a great sense of humour, laconic and irreverent in true Aussie style, but sometimes, he uses it at the wrong times and to the wrong audience.

Not long ago, he was taking a group of Japanese tourists through the outback in a 4WD bus. They drove past a number of large windmills used by station (farm) owners in arid areas to pump water into sheep-and-cattle troughs. One of the Japanese girls pointed at the windmills and asked the guide in broken English, 'Those big machines. What are they for, please?'

Instead of explaining their purpose and giving his clients some insight into station life, an existence so completely different to their own, he responded with sarcasm.

'Well, ya know,' he drawled, 'it gets pretty hot out here. Those things are big fans used to keep the sheep cool.'

Okay, it's kinda funny, but it's not professional, and it's disrespectful to the clients. If any of them retold the story to someone who'd been to Australia, they'd be made to look foolish. Plus, the tour guide wasted a great opportunity to share some interesting information with his group about life in the outback.

3

How Tour Guides Fit into the Tourism Industry

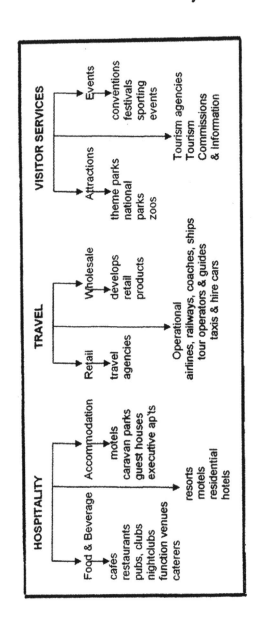

4

Different Types of Tour Guides

There are a number of different types of tours and, consequently, lots of different types of tour guides. There are half-day tours on foot or in vehicles, bicycle, motorbike, or Segway, extended walking tours, cruises, tours in coaches or 4WD vehicles, scenic or themed tours, 'voluntours', and more. Find out what tours are available in your area – you might be surprised at the variety!

Guides Leading Short Tours

These guides usually run short tours lasting from an hour to a half day or a full day. The tours can take place in vehicles or on foot and may be to museums, art galleries, wineries, factories, concert halls, parks, historic buildings, or heritage attractions.

A professional guide leads an award-winning walking tour through the City of Perth. (Photo courtesy Two Feet & a Heartbeat.)

Guides Leading Tours in Coaches

These guides usually work for companies who take clients on one-day tours or extended tours of two or more days' duration with overnight stays. From Perth, coach tours visit such destinations as Margaret River, Wave Rock, or wildflower country, which are likely to be 250 km away or more. The tours usually cover long distances on the bitumen with clients travelling as passengers in vehicles of varying sizes, carrying anywhere from two to forty clients.

Extended tours may also go further afield for anywhere from ten to thirty days or more and cover from 1,000 to 3,000 km. Tours departing from WA may go to such destinations as the Coral Coast, Kimberley, Kakadu, Uluru, or further afield. Coaches usually stay 'on the bitumen'.

On most extended coach tours, clients and staff stay in traditional accommodation such as hotels, motels, or B&Bs (bed and breakfast) and take meals at hotels, restaurants, or cafes.

Sometimes, a coach driver works alone and also acts as a tour guide, but for safety and duty-of-care reasons (particularly with larger groups and when covering long distances), many companies now prefer to employ a driver *and* a tour guide, or two driver/guides, who can share the long hours behind the wheel.

On a coach tour offering camping, clients and staff usually sleep in tents provided by the company and stay in caravan parks with allocated camping areas or in 'bush camps'. If providing the tents, most companies also provide the catering al fresco style, using a catering trailer. In this situation, the company may employ one or more drivers/guides who will also be expected to cook, or they will employ a driver/guide plus a camp cook or hostess.

Luxury tour coaches holding up to forty passengers are used in Australia and overseas for taking large groups on day trips or extended tours. (Photo courtesy Global Gypsies.)

Guides Leading Extended Tours in 4WD Vehicles

In Australia, tour guides working for companies running 'soft adventure' four-wheel-drive (4WD/4x4) tours in remote or outback areas may visit such destinations as Karijini National Park, the Canning Stock Route, the Red Centre, or parts of the Kimberley inaccessible by two-wheel-drive vehicles.

Because of the size of Australia (similar to the USA), these tours cover long distances. Clients and staff are likely to spend many hours on the road on both bitumen and 4WD tracks. Vehicles used on these tours can vary from a standard four-seater 4WD vehicle (such as a Land Cruiser) to a twenty-seater, coach-style 4x4.

As with extended camping tours in coaches, on 4WD tours, accommodation for clients and staff is usually in tents with al fresco catering. The tour operator may employ one or more drivers/guides who will also be expected to cook or will employ a driver/guide *and* a cook.

Large 4×4 overland trucks are used on soft-adventure tours which visit remote areas or destinations inaccessible by two-wheel-drive vehicles. (Photo courtesy Adventure Wild.)

Another type of extended overland expedition is a self-drive tag-along tour in which clients drive their own (or hired) 4×4s and travel in a convoy led by an expert guide communicating by two-way radio. (For more information on how these tours work, visit www.globalgypsies. com.au.)

In addition to running the tour and providing quality narrative, the guide on these tours also needs to have such skills as four-wheel driving, basic mechanics, bush survival, and remote-area first aid. Most tag-along tours are self-catering, but on catered tours, the company provides the meals, usually with a combination of a guide and a cook using a special catering trailer.

Tour Escorts Leading International Tours

Overseas (or outbound) tours are usually undertaken in comfortable coaches or on cruise ships with accommodation and some, or most, meals included. If you accompany an outbound group, once you reach your destination, you will probably be working alongside local English-speaking guides. Companies such as Peregrine, Intrepid, World Expeditions, Global Gypsies and Scenic Tours run these types of tours.

In those instances, your role may be more of a tour 'escort' or 'courier'. Rather than having detailed knowledge of the attractions, culture, and history of a foreign country and providing the commentary, you may be looking after the welfare of the clients, assisting them through customs, expediting hotel check-ins, and ensuring that things generally run smoothly, while the local guide imparts the knowledge about the destination and handles the language problems.

Some Australian-based guides also lead tours to Europe, Africa, Asia, India, Antarctica, or other exotic destinations such as Machu Picchu in Peru, South America. (Photo courtesy Global Gypsies.)

This policy can vary – some tour operators use only local guides/escorts when visiting overseas destinations, while other companies consider that a knowledgeable 'imported' guide is sufficient. Our preference is to have both a local guide *and* an imported tour escort as we believe this combination delivers a higher standard of visitor experience.

From our observations, imparting local knowledge is usually best left to the experts who live there, who know the customs and who speak the language fluently. Also, we find that our clients enjoy the opportunity to interact with a local guide. However, having an imported guide also increases the price of the tour, so this is often only available in more expensive tour products.

Another overseas touring option is extended overland tours in large 4×4 trucks. Usually, these holidays are designed for a younger crowd, cost less than the traditional coach offering, and provide camping and participatory catering. If this kind of tour presses your buttons and you're looking for some adventure in your life, then Africa and South America are the perfect places to work as an overland guide. Companies such as Acacia, African Overland Tours, Dragoman, Intrepid, Odyssey, Peregrine, and Truck Africa are specialists in this field.

Guides Leading Specific Adventure Activity Tours

Both our tour-guide training course and this book cover generic guiding skills; neither addresses specialised adventure tours such as abseiling, canyoning, kayaking, scuba-diving, or equine activities. These tours have very specific requirements on what equipment to carry, what training is required, content of client briefings, tour procedures, and more.

Guides who conduct specific adventure activities *are* closely regulated and *do* require specialised training and licenses in order to operate. For more information on how to become a specialist guide in a specific area of adventure or outdoor activity in Australia, contact the Outdoor Council of Australia (www.outdoorcouncil.asn.au) or the relevant authority where you live.

Although you won't find any advice on specific adventure activities within these pages, the general guiding principles that we've provided will still be invaluable.

Adventure tours such as kayaking have very specific requirements and are closely regulated.
(Photo courtesy Tourism Western Australia/Broome Adventure Company.)

5

Do You Have What It Takes?

We'll go through in detail what it takes to be a good tour guide in subsequent chapters, but before we do, let's find out how much you already know about the profession.

Take a few moments to jot down the skills and characteristics that you believe are required to be an award-winning tour guide. Try to put ten items in each list. You'll have a chance to amend your list and to compare it with the list we've compiled later on. It will be interesting to see if your perceptions change as you learn more about the subject!

Desirable Skills and Knowledge	**Desirable Character Traits**
_____	_____
_____	_____
_____	_____
_____	_____
_____	_____
_____	_____
_____	_____
_____	_____
_____	_____
_____	_____

Now go back and put a tick next to the skills or character traits you think _you_ possess. Do you have what it takes?

6

Day in the Life of a Tour Guide

Different tour companies have different requirements, and depending on what kind of tours you are leading, your days will vary accordingly. But based on the Australian model, here's an idea of what you can expect:

A. Short Tours

Preparation

- Early rise – your alarm clock, watch, or phone alarm is your best friend and worst enemy! Whatever time the tour starts, you need to be there well in advance. And if you're heading out on the road, you'll need to get up with the sparrows!
- Before your day starts, check equipment and paperwork; be familiar with the PA system, first-aid kit, mobile or satellite phone, etc.
- You should be well dressed, well presented, and ready to roll well before you meet the clients.
- First impressions are incredibly important – make a good one!
- Wear a name badge and your company uniform.
- Check the weather forecast by newspaper, Internet, mobile phone, or other means.

- Many guides do temporary work for a number of companies rather than work full-time with one company. If you freelance for several different employers, you need to be *really* organised! Program your iPhone or other electronic device to book in your jobs, or get an old-fashioned diary, day-timer, or other time management tool – and check it regularly!
- You need to have good research skills and a good memory – there's lots to learn and share with your clients! If you aren't already techno-savvy, learn how to use the Internet, particularly Google (remember you'll need a Wi-Fi or G connection to access the net – not always possible in regional or remote areas). Also check out and download the numerous apps on your iPhone, many of which are free. (Again, remember that if they are interactive, you may need a Wi-Fi or G connection to access them).
- Get some good reference books and take them with you on tour – clients ask heaps of questions and enjoy reading the info and looking at the photographs!
- Have your interpretation or narrative prepared and ready to deliver.
- Develop a good delivery style – have a practice run before each session.
- Get comfortable addressing a crowd – you will be doing a lot of public speaking!

During the Tour

- Greet clients as they arrive and make appropriate introductions.
- Count clients at beginning of tour and at each stop, break, or activity. Be sure not to lose anyone!
- Tell clients what to expect on your tour, cover any specific occupational health and safety details, give them housekeeping details such as locations of toilets, emergency exits, etc.
- Wear a seat belt (if available) and ensure that your clients do, too.

- Assist passengers on and off vehicle and with their luggage or gear.
- Watch your timing – you need to cover everything in your itinerary.
- Use the itinerary as your timetable, but be prepared for change if there are unforeseen circumstances.
- Always have a Plan B in case of closed roads, closed venues, bad weather, or other unexpected situations.
- Develop an emergency plan to deal with accidents, illness, fire, or evacuation which may occur during your tour.
- Make sure venues are booked in advance and liaise with venue staff; keep their phone numbers handy, advise them early of any changes to plans. This could be restaurants, motels, campgrounds, or activities such as helicopter rides, cruises, or other things requiring specific group numbers. This is not just to ensure your clients have meals or beds; it's also out of courtesy to other operators or suppliers who could be filling your empty spots with paying customers!
- Warn passengers ten minutes before it's time to get off the coach for an activity or rest stop. Remember that movement of groups always takes longer than you'll expect!
- Give clients a precise time to be back at the vehicle after an activity – build some extra minutes in to allow for stragglers. Explain the timing again clearly to any non-English speaking clients.
- Give clients something to identify the vehicle by – your company logo displayed proudly on the side, license-plate number, scarf on the antenna, bumper sticker, etc.
- During activities in which the group has split up (shopping, for example), find as many clients as you can and give them a reminder that you will be leaving the venue in ten minutes.
- Deliver interpretive commentary and keep it interesting.
- While you're speaking, keep your group sheltered from rain or strong sun. Stand facing the sun so they don't have to! Watch clients' body language and their responses, and adjust your presentation accordingly. Yawning and shuffling amongst the group is not a good sign! If they start getting fidgety,

do something to jazz up your presentation and reclaim their attention – even something a little bit crazy!

B. Longer Tours

On longer tours or extended overland expeditions, in addition to many of the above activities, your day might go like this:

- Early start – be up and about before the clients to boil water, make tea, pack up your own things.
- Eat breakfast – or on an overland tour, you may have to *make* breakfast for the group!
- Break camp, assist clients to pack up their tents and gear.
- You may want to allocate duties to clients to spread the workload. If so, develop a duties roster and put it up on display.
- Wash breakfast dishes and pack them away.
- Check food stocks so you know what needs replenishing.
- Keep fridges and storage boxes clean, tidy, and in hygienic condition.
- Pack away foodstuffs carefully to avoid spills or waste.
- Pack up vehicle and/or trailer with tents, chairs, swags, mattresses, and other equipment – ensuring everything is packed safely and correctly.
- Conduct vehicle checks.
- Do a headcount.
- Once on the road, enforce a fatigue-management plan – stop at least once in the morning and once in the afternoon. for a group comfort stop and to have a break yourself.
- If clients can choose from several optional activities (walks, cruises, joy flights), create a list that shows the price of each activity and names of those who will be participating.
- Visit places of interest, take clients on guided walks or other activities as listed in itinerary, ensuring that all clients have a suitable level of fitness to participate.

- Lunch – know suitable spot with shade, tables. Clean dishes and pack up again.
- You may need to do grocery shopping – either a basic or a big shop. Menus are usually planned in advance, but sometimes, you need to top up your larder. Remember that supplies usually cost more the further you get from the city.
- Arrive at your bush camp, camp ground, or accommodation before dark whenever possible – clients like to 'nest', i.e., set up their tent and sleeping gear.
- On the first day, when you unpack, demonstrate to clients how to use tents, mattresses, swags, chairs, and other gear as they may be unfamiliar with them.
- Ensure clients know kitchen and toileting rules.
- Start preparing dinner.
- During/after dinner, talk about next day's activities and what equipment is needed for each activity (bathing suit, towel, torch for caves, walking shoes, hat, camera, water bottle, and so on).
- Wash and pack up catering gear.
- Lead the conversation around the campfire (if you can have one), organise some games, jokes, music, or other entertainment – somebody in the group usually has hidden talents!
- When clients have gone to bed or you can get some time to yourself, complete vehicle maintenance logs or other reports.
- Shower (if available) – your personal hygiene is vital! Nobody likes a smelly guide! Brush your teeth regularly, and carry gum or mints.
- Sleep – and not with the clients!
- Get up and do it all over again!
- At the end of the tour, thank clients for travelling with you/your company; distribute and collect client-survey forms or other information required.
- Complete any internal paperwork, reconciliations.
- Go home and get some rest so you're bright-eyed and bushy-tailed for your next tour!

Tour Guide Tale #2: The Big-Knife Syndrome

Before we started Global Gypsies, we travelled around Africa writing travel articles. One day, we went on a walking tour with six other tourists in a national park in Zimbabwe. We were looking for elephants in the bush under the supervision of a supposedly professional safari guide. African guides carry guns when they take clients on walking safaris, and our tour guide was no exception. But that wasn't all he carried.

This khaki-clad, testosterone-charged, cocky young guide was decked out like Tarzan. Not only did he have a rifle, but he also had several massive over-the-top knives and numerous other unnecessary gadgets hanging conspicuously off his belt. He was really strutting his stuff, but as we found out later, he was more style than substance and was probably very inexperienced. Truth is, he shouldn't have been leading a walking tour at all where his clients might be exposed to wild animals.

Following his lead, the group quietly approached a water hole and settled in behind some bushes to wait and watch for elephants to come and drink. And come they did! An alpha matriarch and several other mothers and their babies ambled across the savannah to the water's edge just meters away from us. But unfortunately, the herd had walked around us, and the mothers ended up on one side of our group, with their babies on the other side.

African Guiding Rule 101 – never split up babies from their mothers. At that point, it would have been safe for us to retreat. And we should have; we were much too close and in a dangerous position. We signalled to our guide that we should leave, but he insisted that the group should stay to 'get a better view'.

It wasn't long before the huge, imposing matriarch became annoyed by our presence. She trumpeted several times, began flapping her ears ferociously, and thundered towards us in a mock charge to warn us away.

By this time, we were both terrified – we'd been on enough safaris to know that we were in serious danger. The rest of the group were all newbies fresh off the plane; they were just enjoying the excitement of it all, unaware of the extent of the threat.

The elephant rumbled menacingly towards us. The guide, kneeling in front of us, remained rooted to the spot, but by now, his stance was more from fear than from stubbornness. His face was ghostly white, and he was shaking like a leaf. We all just had to stay put and hope for the best.

The matriarch was within metres of us and still coming. To frighten her off, the tour guide stood up suddenly, raised his rifle, and fired a shot in the air. The elephant bellowed in fury and charged again; he fired another shot in the air. This time, thank god, she stopped, kicked up clouds of dust with her huge feet, then turned and stormed angrily back to her family, bellowing, swaying, and shaking her head all the way.

We got the hell out of there as quickly and safely as we could. We retreated slowly backwards, crouching low to the ground and swearing under our breath at the stupidity of the guide. He had endangered the lives of both tourists and animals and ruined this potentially wonderful wildlife encounter for all involved. Had the elephant continued her charge, someone could have suffered serious injury or death. Alternatively, the guide might have had to shoot and kill the animal. Either way, it would have been a horrible outcome and one which could easily have been avoided with a little common sense and a lot less bravado.

We agreed later that the cocky young guide suffered from what we now call the Big-Knife Syndrome – over-confident, under-experienced, and just trying to show off. We reported him to his employers and can only hope he was given a stiff kick up the backside and a lot more training before ever being entrusted with the lives of clients again.

An exciting encounter with wildlife can turn into a disaster in the hands of an inexperienced or poorly trained tour guide. (Photo courtesy Global Gypsies.)

7

Legal Requirements

- Depending on where you live, the type of tour you are running and whether or not you will be transporting clients in a vehicle, you will probably be required by the relevant government transport authority to have a special license to operate that vehicle (light or heavy vehicle driving license, motorcycle license, boat/skipper's ticket). Check for requirements in your area.
- You may also need a special *personal* license from the transport authority in order to carry a specified number of paying or non-paying passengers in your vehicle or vessel (in WA, this is called 'Hire and Reward' or 'F' class license).
- Your vehicle(s) will also probably need to be licensed and meet certain design requirements in order to carry paying passengers with maximum numbers clearly specified. Check on things like specified number of seats, which direction they can face, number and location of doors, and other details.
- Check carefully on the personal and/or company insurance required (public liability, professional indemnity, corporate travel) to cover you and/or your clients in case of accident, injury, or negligence. If working for someone else, find out exactly what their company insurance policy covers, and make sure you are protected as well! Most park authorities require a

minimum amount of between $10–$20-million public liability cover in order to take clients into national parks.

- Even if it's not required legally, you should have a current senior or remote-area first-aid certificate. To be current, the certificate must be renewed regularly – check with your local first-aid training provider for requirements in your area.

- In WA, it has recently been made mandatory for tour companies to be accredited by a recognised tourism body in order to take clients into national parks. To date, this requirement has not been extended to individual tour guides, but this may happen in the future. As a company, we encourage both company and personal accreditation as we believe it helps maintain high professional standards within the industry and delivers a better visitor experience to clients.

- Although there is no legal requirement to undertake independent training, we strongly urge you to do so before you start guiding. This could be an academic qualification, a hands-on commercial course, or on-the-job training run by your employer. You'll find more suggestions in Chapter 29.

8

Knowledge Requirements

If you're working in remote or challenging areas, in addition to the skills we've listed previously, you should have a basic knowledge and understanding of:

- Mechanical skills.
- Fatigue management (in WA, there is a Certificate Program for Bus and Coach Operators).
- Cooking and hygiene (if your company is providing catering).
- Information relevant to all the destinations on your particular tour.
- Flora and fauna,
- Environmental awareness (our corporate environmental policy is included in the back of this book).
- Your responsibilities to park rangers   (information booklets can be obtained from your local parks and/or wildlife authority).
- Duty of care – it is your responsibility to look after your clients. You may have the lives of twenty or more people in your hands! Under the Western Australian Occupational Safety and Health Act 1984, all parties involved have responsibilities for safety and health at work, including employers, employees, self-employed persons, and others. There is probably similar legislation in

your area. As you read on, we will relate examples of situations in which duty of care was demonstrated in both positive and negative ways.

- Safety and risk management, both for your clients and for yourself.
- Information about topics you may be personally interested in, such as geology, astronomy, history, indigenous culture, or whatever.
- 4WD skills – take a 4WD course or join a 4WD club to become a proficient four-wheel driver.
- If you want to lead 4WD tag-along tours, you should take an accredited basic and advanced 4WD course, a basic mechanics course, and a remote-area first-aid course.
- If starting or running your own business, you will need your own appropriate vehicle(s) with relevant licensing plates, suitable equipment in good condition, relevant accreditation (in WA, this is provided by the Department of Transport and the Department of Parks & Wildlife), adequate levels of insurance, plus knowledge of business administration, human resources, marketing, and trip planning. There is a special section devoted to 'Starting Your Own Tour Business' later in this book.

9

Intangible Requirements

Being a tour guide requires a lot of practical abilities, but you also need to possess a whole lot of *intangible* qualities. For example:

- People skills – you could be dealing with a series of small or large groups over short periods, small or large groups over longer periods, or the same group for two weeks or more. If you don't like people, this is not the job for you!
- Extrovert – more people are scared of public speaking than of leaping off a building! But if you're a bit shy when it comes to addressing groups, you'll have to overcome this aversion because you'll be talking to hundreds of people. If it helps, remember that they all want to hear what you have to say and that, in most cases, you'll know way more about the subject than they do.
- Leadership skills – you'll need to be a leader, make decisions, resolve conflicts, establish boundaries, and gain the group's respect not once but every single day.
- Even temperament, no highs and lows – there are no 'bad hair days' for you. You might be like the proverbial duck on the water, smooth on the surface but paddling like crazy underneath, but your clients shouldn't know that! They've paid for a quality visitor experience; it's your job to deliver it no matter what's

going on in your own life. And whatever it is, they don't want to hear about it!

- Patience and tolerance – you need this in spades. Clients can drive you crazy, and you *will* get customer overdose, but just count to 100 and smile.
- Know when you need a rest; ensure you have some down time or rest days between tours.
- Good memory – yep, there's an immense amount to learn and remember.
- Good delivery of your narrative or story – it's no good knowing it if you can't share it.
- Speak clearly, slowly, and project your voice. Narrative is so important that we've devoted a whole chapter to this important aspect of tour guiding later on.
- Don't use sarcasm or slang in your narrative – overseas visitors probably won't get it.
- Show enthusiasm and passion! They're contagious emotions!
- Be caring and understanding. You need to be a SNAG – a sensitive new-age guide!
- Problem-solver – this quality really comes to the fore on longer tours. It might involve resolving personality clashes, finding lost items, sorting out sleeping or food arrangements, or figuring out how to get from point A to point B when confronted by obstacles.
- Amateur psychologist – another quality that becomes more evident on longer tours. What's really going on with your group? How do you keep them interested? How do you bring out the shy ones? Tone down the noisy ones? Help them to bond as a unit?
- Sense of humour – a must. Don't take yourself too seriously, make the group laugh when you can, keep it light. But be sure your jokes aren't insensitive or inappropriate.
- You're always on duty! Be vigilant and alert for safety issues, illness, dehydration, weather, vehicle problems, theft, conflicts between clients, and other potential problems.

10

Personal Gear

Good tour guides should carry their own personal gear, including:

- Copy of relevant itinerary.
- Personal reference books kept in a waterproof/dust-free box.
- First-aid kit.
- Water bottle.
- Folder.
- Pens.
- Calculator.
- Clipboard.
- Stapler.
- Binoculars.
- Torch.
- Leatherman/Swiss army knife.
- Mobile phone and charger (only limited reception in remote areas).
- Satellite phone and charger.
- List of important telephone numbers.
- If on an extended tour, list of emergency contacts for clients.
- Camera/video camera, spare batteries, spare memory cards.

- GPS and/or PLB.
- Laptop computer or iPad.
- Vehicle toolbox.
- Appropriate spare parts and emergency equipment.
- If on a 4WD tour, appropriate 4×4 recovery gear.

11

Appearance

We can't emphasise enough how important that first impression is to setting the tone for your tour! A good tour guide should always:

- Look and act like a professional.
- Wear a uniform and name badge if one is provided.
- Be as well dressed as the best-dressed person on your tour!
- Wear appropriate clothing for your tour. For outdoor or outback work, wear a long-sleeved shirt, short or long pants, covered shoes (boots or hiking shoes, not thongs or tennis shoes), hat, and name badge. Also pack a raincoat, dust coat/overalls, and work gloves in case you have to get under the vehicle to do some repairs or change a tyre.
- For town, if no uniform is provided, wear smart casual clothes with covered shoes; carry a hat, raincoat, and umbrella if you're going to be outdoors.
- Carry your basic generic equipment in a backpack so that your hands are free.
- Carry appropriate equipment for the activity you will be doing – remember that clients will take their cue from you as to what to wear.
- Look tidy – tuck in your shirt!

- Be comfortable but not sloppy.
- Be clean! Comb your hair, brush your teeth, have a shower, wear deodorant, carry emergency 'scrub-up' products and a pack of mints.
- Remember the Big-Knife Syndrome – don't go overboard with gear!

*Jeremy Perks, Global Gypsies Director, Tour Guide and
Senior Trainer, with the company's trusty LandCruiser
(Photo courtesy Global Gypsies.)*

12

Conduct

This section combines some of the things we mentioned before along with some new tips. It's all about conducting yourself like a professional!

- Stick to your timetable; be punctual but flexible.
- Keep clients informed – give regular briefings.
- Again, speak clearly and slowly. Record yourself and listen to how you sound!
- Again, don't use slang. If you have international visitors, they won't understand it.
- Maintain good personal hygiene and health.
- No smoking, drinking, taking illicit drugs, or swearing at any time on your tour.
- Be wary of becoming too friendly with any particular clients during the tour – it will upset the group dynamics.
- Beware of groupies! As a tour leader, you'll have lots of admirers who may be struck with 'khaki fever'. Learn how to deal with the attention politely and sensitively. And don't start believing your own publicity – in a different situation, those clients who see you as Tarzan may not be the least bit interested!
- No sex on the job! You're there to deliver a great experience to the whole group – not just one of them. Everyone will know within

hours about your dalliance no matter how discreet you try to be. Your perceived favouritism will upset the group dynamics, and there could be problems with the person involved if it doesn't work out.

- Be assertive but not dictatorial when controlling the group – it's not a military exercise.
- If you're on a long tour, you'll often have very little advance info about the clients – try to find out about all of them.
- Don't ask the group to make a decision between Options A or B; you'll never get a consensus. You're the boss – you make the decision! They're looking to you for leadership.
- You're likely to have a mix of local, national, and international clients. Try to keep up with current events in states or countries other than your own so that you can carry on an informed conversation about what's happening in their neck of the woods.
- Try to break down cultural barriers – talking with people and getting to know them is the best way to do this.
- Be observant and intuitive.
- Be patient and tolerant. Clients may ask what you consider to be really dumb questions, but remember this is their first time here – you've been here heaps of times!
- Be innovative, know how to improvise – always have a Plan B to deal with bad weather, no wildlife, no wildflowers, closed facilities, flooded roads, need to change itinerary, vehicle repairs, etc.
- If there's a problem, complaint, or disagreement, don't argue with a client. 'Yes, you did,' 'No, I didn't,' is a dead-end street. Be rational, logical, and keep emotion out of the discussion.
- If things do get heated, don't get physical – be assertive, not aggressive. You need to stay cool, calm, and be in control at all times. If the situation comes to blows, it's probably either time that the person left the tour or that you stopped being a tour guide!
- Have a good attitude – not too slack or too cool.

- Be happy and positive – no doom and gloom or black clouds for you!
- Show enthusiasm, excitement, passion! You may have been to this destination dozens of times, but this is probably your clients' very first visit! Keep the experience fresh and exciting. (Want some inspiration? Go on to the web site of rock artist Pink and listen to her explain how she gets revved up before each concert. She focuses on just *one* person in the audience that she wants to make happy!)
- Under-promise – over-deliver.
- Be proud of your profession! *You are special and highly skilled!*

13

Problem-Solving

If you're a tour guide, you'll need to also be a problem-solver, and if you're leading longer tours, you are likely to have more problems to solve than on shorter ones. Here are some tips to help you out.

Solve problems while they're tiny to avoid them becoming bigger, but unless it's an emergency, you usually don't have to come up with a solution *immediately*. If the situation allows it, take some time to think the problem through and consider a range of solutions, and consult any other relevant parties if necessary.

Sometimes, you'll be able to make your own decision as to how to solve a particular problem; sometimes, you might like to ask the group for their input. If you're working for someone else, depending on the severity and nature of the problem, you may also need to involve your employer in the decision-making process.

When deciding how to resolve the problem, first describe or outline the situation to yourself (or others if they are involved in the decision-making process). Then list the possible solutions and the pros and cons of each (in business, this is called a SWOT analysis, in which you consider the strengths, weaknesses, opportunities, and threats of each course of action).

Once you've come to a conclusion, act on it decisively, and implement the action with authority. Remember that you need to demonstrate calmness and clear thinking – the group is looking to you for leadership and a solution!

Before you embark on your tour, find out your employer's company policy on a range of possible scenarios. There may also be particular paperwork which needs to be completed in these situations which you should carry with you. And if you're starting up (or are already running) your own tourism business, develop your own company policies and documentation. Here are some problems and possible solutions that you may be faced with one day:

Q. What happens if a client demands to leave your tour and wants his or her money back?

A. *Listen to the problem. Are the client's gripes legitimate? If you work for someone else, discuss the issue with your employer – don't offer a refund without getting their agreement first. If it's your company, make a decision based on the policy you've developed.*

Q. What's the procedure for dealing with a client who becomes seriously ill or injured while on your tour? Who do you need to contact?

A. *Your first-aid training will help you deal with the medical aspects of this one. The severity of the situation will also help you decide on the best course of action.*

The client may need to be evacuated, so have the contact details handy of emergency services and the Royal Flying Doctor Service. Also remember the magic numbers, 000 and 112! Before you depart on your tour, make sure that next-of-kin details appear on all client-booking forms in case you need to contact a client's relatives in an emergency.

Q. What's the correct procedure to follow if someone dies while on your tour?

A. *This is usually a matter for the police in the region where the death occurred – most rescue and/or evacuation services won't assist once a person is deceased, only when they are injured or ill.*

Best not to move the deceased (unless you need to do so for safety or hygienic reasons). Stay with the body and cover it with a sheet, blanket, or some other suitable material. Take careful notes of what happened, as you and others in the group will probably be interviewed later. Sounds gory, but take some photographs for the record. And, of course, comfort the others in the group, particularly relatives of the deceased. Be aware that others in the group may go into shock – you'll need to deal with that as a first-aid issue. Then wait for the police to arrive.

Q. What's the correct procedure to follow if your vehicle is involved in an accident?

A. *Again, this is a police matter with specific steps to follow and standard documentation to complete. Your first priority should be to check for injuries in your own and the other vehicle. If anyone needs assistance, and you are a trained first-aider (which you should be), go into first-aid mode. Once police and an ambulance (if necessary) have been called, phone your employer, as it is likely there will be insurance or vehicle repair and possibly tour-rescheduling issues he/she will need to address. Take careful notes, and take photos for the record.*

Q. What's the correct procedure to follow if you witness an accident or if you discover an accident involving other people while on tour?

A. *If there are injuries, and you are a trained first-aider, follow your training procedures. However, remember the primary responsibility you have for your own group and their safety and well-being. Take careful notes, and take photos for the record.*

Q. What happens if you, the tour guide, become sick or injured and cannot complete the tour?

A. *You and/or your employer need to develop a clear contingency plan for this. Some companies are able to provide a substitute employee on short notice; smaller companies may not have this option. If you fall into the latter category, have a list handy of other guides you can contact in an emergency.*

In some instances when guides have become ill or injured, they have asked one of the clients to assist them or act as a temporary leader until more formal arrangements can be implemented.

Or it may be necessary to cancel the tour altogether, which then opens another can of worms, what with arranging client transport to the closest town, assisting them with onward travel arrangements, considering refunds, etc.

In other more serious cases, a client has stepped up and completely taken over the leadership role out of necessity. One tragic incident occurred when a group of European tourists were enjoying a lengthy guided canoe tour in Africa. They were paddling in a quiet and remote section of the Zambezi River when a large hippo suddenly surfaced and attacked the lead canoe.

The boat tipped over, and the hippo then turned its attention to the people in the water. The tour guide was killed trying to protect his clients. The tourists had to deal with the emergency themselves, find shelter, and get themselves back to civilisation. It took them several days, but they were successful because a leader with basic bush-survival skills emerged from the group and took control.

Q. How should you deal with an individual who has a problem with your tour or is causing problems and dissatisfaction amongst the other clients?

A. *We find that the best course of action is to take the individual aside and discuss the issue privately on a one-on-one basis to try to find a solution. If* *the person has a legitimate complaint about you or the tour, see if you can improve the situation for them.*

If you have a complaint about the person, tell them honestly but tactfully, and try to come to an understanding about their behaviour.

If your solutions to either of these situations don't work, you may want to consider asking the client to leave the tour, particularly if their attitude or behaviour is affecting the enjoyment of the tour for other clients.

Q. Under what circumstances can you ask a client to leave your tour?

A. *There are no hard and fast rules here. You and/or your employer need to develop your own guidelines on where you draw the line and how to deal with a client who is, for example, using drugs, over-indulging in alcohol, stealing, behaving in ways which upset other tour participants, causing damage to persons or property, or disregarding your instructions for safe conduct of the tour. Depending on the situation, you may need to involve your employer, local police, park officials, or other authorities.*

Know what steps to take once you make the decision to ask a client to leave your tour. Be calm, polite, firm but not aggressive, and make the request in private. Follow your request through in a decisive fashion with regard for the impact the decision may have on the other clients. Depending on the situation, or if the client becomes aggressive, you may need to involve your employer, local police, park officials, or other authorities.

Q. What happens if clients try to take over a tour?

A. *You have to know how to handle a mutiny – seriously! Several years ago, we heard about an extended – and very unhappy! – overland tour in Africa in which the clients mutinied! For a week or more, they had made numerous complaints to the company's management about their guide, whom they said was lazy, rude, incompetent, unfamiliar with the route, and a bad driver.*

When the company ignored their complaints, the outraged clients kicked the hapless tour guide off the bus, left him by the side of the road in a remote African village, commandeered the vehicle, appointed a leader from the group, and continued the tour on their own!

Hopefully, this will never happen to you because, after you read this book, you'll be an award-winning guide! But if you ever do sense rumblings of dissatisfaction from your clients, nip the problem in the bud – discuss and resolve the problem early on, before a mob mentality sets in.

As an exercise, list some other challenging situations on which a tour company should have a clearly defined policy:

_____

_____

_____

_____

Happy clients enjoy sundowners after a day of 4WD fun on the Lancelin sand dunes near Perth. (Photo courtesy Global Gypsies.)

Tour Guide Tale #3: Counting Heads!

A group of tourists went scuba-diving on the Great Barrier Reef with a commercial tour operator. The dive boat took them to an exquisite dive spot 50+ km from the mainland known for its colourful fish and coral.

You would assume that the tour operator did a headcount when everyone boarded the boat and before they got into the water. You would also assume that the divers were given a specific time to surface and return to the boat.

As expected, the diving was fantastic. But in the excitement, nobody noticed that two divers, a married couple, had stayed down longer than they should have and had not surfaced with the rest of the group.

When the boat began its preparations to head back to the mainland, it is alleged that staff members may not have done an accurate headcount. Consequently, nobody realised that the two divers were missing. The boat returned to port without them.

The tourists were left behind in the open sea. It is alleged that more than twenty-four hours elapsed before a crew member found two dive bags on the boat and pushed the panic button. A massive search was undertaken, but their bodies were never found.

There was much controversy as to whether their disappearance was an accident or was a planned murder/suicide. Either way, accurate headcounts before, during, and after the dive could have uncovered the problem and possibly have prevented this tragedy.

14

Duty of Care

Duty of care is a moral or legal obligation to ensure the safety or well-being of others. As a tour guide, you have the safety, well-being, and, in some cases, the lives of a number of human beings in your hands. This means you have a duty of care and responsibility for:

- Your passengers/clients/customers.
- The vehicle you are driving/hiring.
- The equipment you are using.
- The venue(s) you are visiting.
- The environment in general.
- Your employer's reputation.

You also have a responsibility to and are an unofficial ambassador for:

- Your state/city/province.
- Your country.
- The tourism industry as a whole.

You also have a responsibility and duty of care for yourself! Without you, the tour can't happen!

- Sleep is one of the most important bodily functions and requirements. It is particularly important for coach drivers and drivers/guides.
- Try to get a good night's sleep and maintain a regular sleep pattern.
- Eat well.
- Stay hydrated.
- Try to exercise.
- Stay off the booze and drugs!
- Fatigue contributes to poor decision-making, inferior judgment, and accidents!
- Have a fatigue-management plan. Include rest stops in your daily planner; know when you are starting to feel fatigued and what to do about it (pause the trip to take a walk, visit an attraction, check the tyres, share the driving if there is a second driver, and so on). Remember that fatigue affects the body in similar ways to alcohol and is responsible for numerous traffic accidents.

15

Risk Management/Occupational Health and Safety

The official definition of risk management is 'the identification, assessment, and prioritisation of risks followed by coordinated and economical application of resources to minimise, monitor, and control the probability and/or impact of unfortunate events or to maximise the realisation of opportunities'.

Part of your duty of care is to have sound risk-management plans and to be aware of, and comply with, current occupational health-and-safety regulations in your workplace and on tour. These vary from place to place, but here are some basic guidelines:

- Have clearly defined and, ideally, written risk-management strategies. It's best to prevent a problem rather than have to deal with it afterwards. (If you or your company is accredited, the accreditation body may provide templates for a range of risk-management scenarios.)
- Consider how to evacuate your vehicle in case of emergency; make sure your clients know this as well.
- Know first-aid – take a course with a reputable organisation such as St John's or Red Cross, and keep your certificate current.

If you're heading into remote areas, upgrade your qualification to remote-area first-aid or equivalent.

- Have a first-aid kit, fire extinguisher, and emergency communications equipment handy. Make sure that it is all in good working order and that you know how to use it. If you're working for someone else, make sure your employer provides this equipment and checks it regularly.
- Know how to contact emergency services – keep a list of important phone numbers handy.
- Try to find out in advance if any of your clients suffer from any allergies or medical conditions – this information should be provided on their booking forms.
- Identify and counsel unfit/unhealthy clients as to which activities (in your professional opinion as a tour guide) they should/should not do while on your tour.
- Know the risks and possible dangers of the areas you are visiting, and advise your clients accordingly. Ignorance can breed disaster!
- Know where you're going, allow enough time to complete the route, and take the proper equipment with you for the activity.
- Do headcounts – not once but often! Before you know it, someone can wander away from your group to take a photo, look at a flower, whatever. If you're in an outback or forest situation, this can be a recipe for disaster as it's so easy to become disoriented. Some guides appoint an assistant headcounter for the duration of the tour or use other techniques. However you check your client numbers, do it regularly and systematically. Don't lose anyone during your watch!
- Make and follow rules about appropriate client behaviour (national parks usually have codes of client and staff behaviour that you can use as thought starters or even as printed handouts).
- Give clear instructions to your clients at the outset as to how you expect them to behave while on your tour.
- Consider how you will respond if a client deliberately disobeys your instructions and insists on putting himself/herself at risk (this can be due to alcohol, drugs, bravado, or perhaps not

understanding your instructions clearly). You cannot force a client to behave sensibly or to do what he or she is told, and there have been occasions when clients deliberately disobeyed a tour guide's instructions with unfortunate results (swimming while intoxicated, walking in the bush after dark, going off alone when instructed to stay with others are some examples).

One possible way to deal with this situation is, if you have already delivered the appropriate warnings and explained the inherent risks to the individual with no success, go through the process again, this time in the presence of other clients (witnesses!). Try to get the individual to publicly state his intention to disobey your instructions and to accept the risks in front of these witnesses or even record the discussion on a smart phone. Hopefully, common sense will prevail, but if you cannot prevent him or her from taking action that could cause harm to himself or others, if an accident does happen and a lawsuit ensues, at least you can prove that you did your best to deliver a high level of duty of care.

- Have appropriate insurance cover – tour guides can be held personally responsible for a client's injury or death.
- Know your duty of care to all parties to whom you are responsible (refer to previous section on this topic) and always demonstrate it!
- Show good judgment – consider local weather conditions, local road conditions, and other factors which could affect the safety of your tour.
- Ensure that all clients have signed appropriate disclaimer forms before they join your tour.

Here's the Terms and Conditions form we had drawn up by a lawyer for Global Gypsies – feel free to use it as a template, incorporating amendments as needed for your own tours. Read it carefully, and pay particular attention to points 39 and 40 – these alone could save your bacon one day!

Global Gypsies Terms and Conditions

GLOBAL GYPSIES PTY. LTD.

General Responsibilities and Duty of Care

1. Global Gypsies (GG) will use its best endeavours and make every effort to operate all tours and training programs as advertised.
2. I/we understand that GG and/or its agents operate in remote areas. GG reserves the right to amend, vary, re-route or cancel an adventure itinerary where, in its best judgement, road, climatic, or other circumstances deem it to be necessary.
3. GG cannot guarantee exact arrival and departure times.
4. GG reserves the right to employ guides and trainers other than those advertised should the need arise.
5. At the discretion of GG, a tour or training program may not proceed if minimum numbers are not achieved. GG shall advise you as soon as possible should an adventure not proceed under this clause.
6. GG discourages young children from participating on GG tours and training programs unless stipulated as taking place during school holidays.
7. No pets are permitted on any GG tours or training programs.
8. I/we understand and accept that GG tours and training programs are challenging, self-sufficient experiences.
9. I/we agree to observe the safety and other instructions of the authorised tour leader/guide/trainer for the duration of the tour or training program.
10. I/we understand and accept that GG, its employees, subsidiaries and agents, is not itself a carrier or hotelier, does not make flight bookings, nor does it own aircraft or hotels. GG takes every care in the selection of carriers, hotels, coach operators, driver/guides, travel agents and the suppliers of hire vehicles and other travel services used in adventure tours (all of which are hereafter referred to as 'the other suppliers').
11. I/we understand and accept that all bookings made with GG are subject to the terms and conditions and limitations and liability imposed by the other suppliers, some of whom limit or exclude liability in respect to death, personal injury or delay.

12. I/we understand and accept that GG is not in any way liable for the acts, omissions or default whether negligent or otherwise, of the other suppliers.

13. While every care and precaution is taken, I/we understand that GG is not liable for the sickness or injury of any participant.

14. I/we confirm that we do not have any pre-existing medical condition or disability which will impact on or prevent me/us from participating in or completing this tour or training program.

15. Where a tour or training program is carried out in an area without proper medical services, GG and its servants and agents are expressly authorised by me/us and each participant for whom we are responsible to take such action as is necessary for the provision of medical services. This shall include, but not be limited to, the arrangement of any medical evacuation service by air/road, the attendance of any doctor/nurse, and any necessary hospital service.

16. I/we understand that all associated costs of the provision of medical services as specified in Clause 15 are to be borne by me/us.

17. GG strongly recommends that you take out a comprehensive travel insurance policy including medical evacuation coverage, cancellation and theft of personal property in order for you to be indemnified against any losses for which you would otherwise be liable under this agreement.

Tag-Along Tours

18. For logistical and safety reasons, a tag-along convoy organised by GG can comprise no more than twelve vehicles (plus guide).

19. I confirm that I and any co-drivers possess a driver's license valid in Australia.

20. I/we accept full responsibility for the maintenance of my/our vehicle during the safari. This includes regularly checking water, battery and oil levels and tyre pressures.

21. I/we understand that 'tag-along-tours' are challenging self-drive adventures traversing remote areas.

22. I/we understand that the tour price does not include the cost of any vehicle repairs or towing expenses.

23. I/we understand that we will be liable for all traffic offences incurred during the safari.

24. It is understood that in the event that GG arranges/facilitates hire of vehicles or other equipment for a client, the contract and terms and conditions for use of that equipment is between the client and the supplier of the goods.

25. GG recommends that you have some form of vehicle insurance (in addition to third party).

26. Hire vehicles and/or equipment must be paid for prior to collection.

Booking and Cancellation Policy

27. To make a booking, client/agent must provide Global Gypsies (GG) with written, faxed or e-mailed instructions along with a 10 per cent non-refundable deposit payable to Global Gypsies by bank/business cheque, international money order, or credit card (Visa or Master Card) and posted to PO Box 123, Scarborough, WA, 6922, Australia or faxed to 618 9205 1330. A booking is accepted on the issue of written confirmation by GG.

28. On trips of seven days or more, deposit must be received by GG a minimum of ninety days prior to departure. On weekend trips, receipt of deposit is at the discretion of GG.

29. On extended safaris, the final balance of the specified amount payable for the adventure is due sixty days prior to departure (ninety days for some overseas tours). If a booking is made within thirty days prior to departure, then payment in full must accompany the booking.

30. In the case of any cancellation prior to commencement by GG, GG will offer a full refund of monies paid less expenses, or try to include you on a subsequent adventure.

31. Should it be necessary for you to cancel your tour or training session, you must notify GG immediately in writing. The notification will take effect the day it is received by GG. Monies will be refunded less incurred administration costs as set out in the schedule below:

Number of days before departure:	(this may vary on overseas tours)
More than sixty days	Loss of deposit
59–41 days	40 per cent of package price
40–31 days	60 per cent of package price
30 days or less	No refund

32. At GG's discretion, if your place can be filled by another full-paying client prior to the trip departure date, GG will refund your money in full, minus the deposit and incurred administration costs. We recommend you take out travel insurance to cover this possibility.

33. The non-issuance of an invoice or the non-payment and/or non-receipt of an invoice will not exempt participants from the cancellation penalties contained herein.

Legal Considerations

34. Neither GG, its Tour Leaders, trainers or other persons or organisations associated with training or tuition accept any liability for any damage to any persons or property resulting from the subsequent action of participants.

35. These terms and conditions are incapable of alteration or waiver by a servant, agent or representative of GG or by any other supplier.

36. I give my permission for GG to use any digital, film or video photographs they may take of me, my family or my vehicle, in their advertising, or web site. NB. If you do not wish your images to be used, please cross out and initial this paragraph.

37. 37 I/we give permission to GG to provide our names, addresses and phone numbers to other participants on this tour or training session, however, GG will not disclose my/our personal details to any other party without prior permission.

38. Notwithstanding anything contained in this Agreement to the contrary, GG shall not be liable for any loss, injury, delay, damage or other casualty suffered or incurred by you due to storms, fires, earthquakes, explosions, embargoes, Government directives, or any other law or regulation, litigation or labour dispute, act of God, war, terrorism, or any other cause which is beyond our reasonable control.

39. This Agreement is and shall be governed by and construed in accordance with the law of the State of Western Australia.

40. Any legal conflict which may arise under this Agreement shall be resolved in the legal jurisdiction of Western Australia.

I/we understand and agree to the Terms and Conditions set out on both pages of this agreement.

Name (Please print): _____

Signed: _____ (Date) _____

Name (Please print): _____

Signed: _____ (Date) _____

Tour Guide Tale #4: Know the Risks and Act Accordingly

A small private party was holidaying on a commercial charter boat in the remote and tropical Kimberley region of North West Australia. The area is known to be frequented by saltwater crocodiles, so swimming is not encouraged except in a few restricted areas.

The boat was moored in a scenic billabong (or pool) with a lovely waterfall. The captain had allegedly told his clients not to swim there, but spirits were high, apparently alcohol had been consumed, the day was hot, the water was tempting, and two of the girls dived in.

They swam around happily for several minutes. Suddenly, a huge crocodile appeared. The captain shouted at the girls to get out of the water and onto nearby rocks. Instead, one of the girls panicked and tried swimming to the boat. The crocodile attacked, and she was killed.

People who knew the area well said the captain should have been aware of the dangers and should have done everything in his power to prevent his clients from going into the water. If that is so, then the clients paid a high price for what may have been either a lack of knowledge, poor judgement, or failure to follow the captain's instructions.

Should the captain have exercised his authority more assertively? Should he have been more concerned about risk management and his duty of care? Incidents like this raise interesting ethical questions as to just how far a tour guide can go to ensure that clients follow instructions.

Saltwater crocodiles can lurk unseen in tranquil billabongs (pools) and rivers in tropical areas of Australia. Tour guides are responsible for the safety and well-being of their clients and must demonstrate the highest levels of duty of care. (Photo courtesy Global Gypsies.)

16

Dealing with Emergencies

If you find yourself in an emergency situation, follow these rules:

- Take a deep breath; stay calm and in control – keep a cool head.
- Assess the situation.
- Know emergency procedures and policies.
- Know the location of emergency exits for the premises or vehicle.
- Have a list of emergency contacts easily accessible or on display where everyone can see them.
- Keep your first-aid knowledge current.
- Know where the necessary emergency and communications equipment is located.
- Know how to deal with a traffic accident whether or not your vehicle is involved.
- Know how to deal with a medical problem, sickness, or injury – to clients or *you*.
- Have the occasional drill – even if it's a mental one!

After the emergency you should:

- Prepare a brief report.
- Get contact details from witnesses.

- Inform your employer; get further instructions from him or her.
- Hold a debrief with your group.
- If the emergency has caused a delay in your schedule, work out how you are going to get back on track.
- Reassure your clients.
- Reinforce confidence in your leadership, and get on with the job.

17

Leadership and Team Building

In order to be an award-winning tour guide, especially on an extended group tour, you need to be a good leader. You need to know how to build a team, develop loyalty, and create a sense of camaraderie. Here are some pointers on leadership and team building (some of which we've touched on previously):

- Lead by example – walk the walk; don't just talk the talk.
- Know what you're talking about.
- Be consistent.
- Be honest.
- Be someone your clients can trust and respect.
- Inspire the group – your positive and enthusiastic attitude will be the foundation of the tour.
- Make decisions calmly and with all the facts.
- Solve problems logically.
- Implement solutions decisively.
- Always keep a cool head.
- Be patient and tolerant.
- Keep your sense of humour.
- Encourage bonding and participation.

- Be observant and intuitive – learn how to read people and situations.
- Support the weaker members of the group – draw them out and get them involved.
- Make everyone in your group feel important and valued.
- Remember that you can't demand respect from your clients – you have to earn it.

18

Environmental Awareness

As a tour guide, you have a responsibility to look after the environment in which you work, particularly if, like us, your office is in the great outdoors! Here are some ways to do this:

- Know and implement your employer's environmental policy (or if it's your own company, develop your own policy).
- Consider getting eco-accreditation with Ecotourism Australia (or similar organisation in your area) either on a corporate or personal level.
- Consider ways you and/or your company can offset the carbon footprint of your tours.
- Consider how you could improve your tours to minimise any possible environmental damage.
- On extended tours, get clients to help you with clean-ups – this not only benefits the environment, it makes your customers more environmentally responsible as well and makes them feel as if they are doing their bit.

You may also want to take out personal and/or corporate memberships in such eco-friendly organisations as Trackcare, Ecotourism Association,

Wildlife Warriors, World Wildlife Fund, Greenpeace, Bush Heritage, etc. (or similar organisations in your area).

Perhaps, like us, you'll want to adopt an animal through the David Sheldrick Wildlife Trust in Kenya (http://www.sheldrickwildlifetrust. org) the Orangutan Trust in Borneo, or other wildlife or conservation organisation (donations over a certain amount to registered fundraising organisations are usually tax deductible).

We were the first tag-along tour company (self-drive tour led by an escort vehicle) in Western Australia to develop and implement an environmental policy. We've printed it here. Feel free to use it with modifications to suit your tour or circumstances.

GLOBAL GYPSIES PTY. LTD.

Global Gypsies
Environmental and Sustainability
Management Policy

Environmentally Responsible 4WD Practices

- Use only approved 4WD tracks; never drive on virgin sand dunes or areas of reclamation, reforestation or revegetation.
- Emphasise environmental awareness at the pre-Departure Workshop and include a copy of this Environmental Management Policy in each Pre-Departure Kit.
- Emphasise environmental awareness to clients at every opportunity.
- Demonstrate responsible environmental practices when four wheel driving, i.e., if bogged, dig the vehicle out, don't churn up tracks, be careful not to damage approaches or exit points or make 'bow waves' when making river crossings, remove obstacles from tracks, etc.
- Obtain relevant approvals in advance for any areas we intend to visit over which they have jurisdiction; advise clients of their responsibilities while in these areas.
- Obtain relevant approvals in advance for any Aboriginal Reserves we intend to visit; advise clients of their responsibilities while in these areas.
- Drive at a reasonable and safe speed to suit conditions and conserve fuel – no racing through river crossings or bush tracks as the macho heroes do on the TV commercials!
- Limit number of vehicles in each convoy to minimize impact on bush tracks, bush camps and surrounds.
- Only tow caravans or camper trailers on suitable roads and tracks.

Environmentally Responsible Waste Disposal

- Ensure clients never throw rubbish from their vehicles; include 'Keep Australia Beautiful' car rubbish bags in Pre-Departure Kits.
- Encourage clients to leave their campsite neat and tidy on departure.

- Use designated camp grounds/caravan parks whenever possible.
- When making bushcamps, encourage clients to dig their 'bush toilets' at least 100 m downwind from camp and at least ½ metre deep using the shovel provided, and to use biodegradable toilet paper. Alternatively have clients burn toilet paper in the campfire (when possible) so that it is not dug up and scattered by wild animals.
- Provide soak pits for run-off water from showers, hand basins, dishwashing and food preparation when in bush camps.
- Remove all rubbish from camp and dispose of it prior to departure in the facilities provided. If bush camping, take rubbish out and dispose of it in appropriate town bins.
- Squash cans for easier transport and disposal.
- Divide rubbish for recycling purposes whenever possible.

Environmentally Responsible Resource Management

- Use biodegradable soap, dishwashing liquid and shampoo when bush camping and encourage clients to do the same.
- Take adequate water supplies along; try not to deplete water supplies in remote areas.
- Do not allow clients to bathe with soap, shampoo hair or wash clothes or dishes in rivers, lakes or the ocean.
- Encourage clients to bring cardboard casks of wine rather than bottles
- Do not light campfires out of season.
- When building a campfire in season, build it only in a small enclosed space in the designated area and using the firepit facilities provided.
- Fires should be built away from trees and dry bush, extinguished with water at night, and checked before breaking camp. If building a campfire in season, bring own wood, use only wood provided or gather dead wood trying not to damage undergrowth or live bush.
- Only make fire big enough to do the necessary cooking or socialising – no big bonfires.
- Recycle paper in the Global Gypsies office for notes, messages, etc.
- Capture and re-use as much grey water as possible in the GG home/office.
- Choose recycled paper for stationery and business cards.
- Use e-mails when possible to minimise paper usage.

Environmentally Responsible Vehicle Maintenance

- Any disposable fluids from vehicle maintenance operations (oil, transmission fluid, etc.) to be stored in appropriate containers until reaching appropriate town disposal facilities.
- Ensure that own and client vehicles comply with vehicle emissions standards.

Respecting the Landscape, Flora, Fauna, History and Culture

- Research the areas we intend to visit in order to provide clients with as much information as possible about the local landscape, flora, fauna, history and culture
- Show respect for the local culture and environment.
- Incorporate local guest speakers in the program wherever possible so they can share their localised knowledge of history, culture, flora, fauna and environmental issues
- Purchase fuel and supplies in areas we visit so that we make a sustainable contribution to local communities.
- No pets are allowed on Global Gypsies safaris as they can damage the flora and fauna and are not permitted entry into parks and reserves (our Dog-Along Tours are restricted to dog-friendly areas and do not enter national parks).
- Discourage clients from approaching, touching or feeding wild birds or animals unless instructed to do so by the Guide.
- Discourage clients from taking souvenirs such as wildflowers, coral, shells, rocks, fossils, etc from areas they visit. Take only photographs and memories!
- Leave property, gates and equipment as we found them.
- Look out for small animals on the road, and if possible, stop the tour and remove them from danger.
- Provide assistance to other travellers wherever possible.

***

Tour Guide Tale #5: Prepare for Your Tour

Karijini National Park in North Western Australia is like a mini version of the Grand Canyon. It's known for its challenging canyons and gorges and is a popular place for hikers and abseilers.

One day, a tour guide led a group into remote country on a walking tour. They were supposed to be back at camp by sunset but became lost, allegedly due to the guide's inexperience and lack of familiarity with the route. Darkness fell, and the guide was unable to find his way out. He was not carrying a satellite phone so had no way to communicate with authorities.

The tourists had to spend the night at the bottom of the gorge in freezing temperatures with little food, no shelter, and no warm clothing. The situation was already dire enough, but during the ordeal, one of the clients fell and was badly injured.

The next day, someone from the campground alerted authorities that the group had not returned to their tents. A massive search was mounted by volunteers and Aboriginal trackers on foot, in vehicles, and in helicopters. The group was found and escorted out by the fabulous folks from the State Emergency Service (SES).

However, a separate and very complicated exercise was needed to rescue the injured tourist from the bottom of the gorge and winch him up to the top of the canyon. A brave SES volunteer abseiled down to attempt the risky manoeuvre. He reached the bottom, but then, without warning, a flash flood suddenly roared through the gorge. The heroic SES worker was drowned.

Several months later, a coronial inquiry was held. Although Jeremy hadn't been present at the incident, he was invited to appear as an expert witness because of his experience as an outback guide and his extensive knowledge of the area. He testified that, in his professional opinion, had the tour guide been more knowledgeable, better prepared, better equipped, more experienced, and more professional, the tragedy could have been prevented.

After all the evidence had been presented, the coroner ruled that the death had been by misadventure and recommended that the state government look more closely at accreditation.

Spectacular Karijini National Park in remote North West Australia is the scene of numerous walking and climbing accidents because of the rugged terrain and deep gorges. Ensure your clients are adequately prepared, watch them carefully, brief them thoroughly, stay within designated safe walking areas, and know how to handle an emergency. (Photo courtesy Global Gypsies.)

19

Preparation and Administration

Each company has its own procedures and policies for tour preparation and administration, but here are some general guidelines:

- Checklists – most companies have these to help you prepare for each tour. If not, create your own so you don't forget anything.
- Passenger list – should include, as a minimum, client names, emergency contacts, health issues, food allergies, and nationality.
- Written itineraries and trip notes about the places you will be visiting.
- Checklist of vehicle, emergency equipment, fire extinguishers, emergency exits.
- Checklist of other equipment you may need to carry – tables, chairs, tents, cooking equipment, food, etc.
- Food-purchasing policies – if you are providing catering on your tour, you will usually depart with a full stock of food, but find out about restocking policies once you are on the road.
- Forms of payment – if you are using other suppliers along the way (hotels, restaurants, campgrounds, grocery stores, fuel stations, and so on), how will you be paying for purchases? Make sure you have the necessary credit cards (with authority for your use), vouchers, petty cash, or other methods of payment.

- Company documentation – you will probably be expected to keep accurate records of expenditures, vehicle use, vehicle maintenance, accident reports, and so on. Be prompt and accurate with this documentation, and do it daily! Don't make the mistake of trying to complete records at the end of your trip; you're sure to forget something important or suddenly find that your finances don't balance!

20

Time Management

Timing is crucial to a tour. Here are some timely tips!

- Wear a watch!
- Each company will have their own itinerary, and it's usually tight. Know it, and stick to it!
- Learn how to move your clients along without making them feeling rushed.
- Build time in for 'people moving' – it always takes longer to move a group than an individual.
- Be prompt and punctual – plan well and be creative and flexible
- Work smarter not harder; get up a bit earlier, but no speeding when driving!
- Tell your clients how long they have to undertake each activity and give them a set time to return. Build in a bit of a buffer – we cannot emphasise enough that things take longer with groups.
- Include rest stops in your daily planning.

21

Setting Up a Bush Camp

If your tour involves camping, you and your clients need to have special knowledge about how to camp responsibly and protect the environment while enjoying the outdoor experience. Here are some valuable tips:

A. Responsible campers should practice the seven Leave No Trace principles:

- Plan ahead and prepare.
- Travel and camp on durable surfaces.
- Dispose of waste properly.
- Leave what you find.
- Minimise campfire impacts.
- Respect wildlife.
- Be considerate of your hosts, park rangers, and other campers.

B. Here's a step-by-step guide to setting up your camp:

- Select your campsite. If there are designated areas, use them. If there are no designated areas, choose sites which will have minimal environmental impact but will be comfortable and have minimal risk. Consider such factors as trees with overhanging branches which could fall and damage a tent or injure its occupants, dry river beds which could suddenly fill, roads or tracks which may not be in use now but could be used unexpectedly by a 4WD or trail bike, lights, noise levels (generators, noisy neighbours, etc.), and proximity to water, toilets, and other facilities. Also consider prevailing winds, type of surface, slopes, rocks, tree stumps, anthills, proximity to fire or smoke, privacy, and sun and moon positions.

- When building a fire, always use existing fire rings (when available). Consider wind direction for possible flying sparks, don't put tents or possessions too close to the fire, ensure there is no danger to people or environment, keep the fire small, don't leave it burning briskly overnight, and douse it thoroughly when you leave – make sure it cannot reignite and cause a wildfire.

- If there are no fire rings, build a small fire in a pit well away from overhanging trees and other flammable objects, and surround it by rocks (if available) to contain it within a small area.

- Do not throw bottles, tins, or aluminium foil in the fire as they will not burn and will just leave a mess for the next campers.

- Bring your own firewood or use only dead wood for your fire. Don't decimate the area close to the campground for firewood; try to look further afield. Some commercial campgrounds sell firewood for this purpose.

- Don't take souvenirs from the campsite (flowers, shells, stones, etc.).

- Develop and implement a rubbish disposal policy. If the site has rubbish bins provided, use them, and ensure lids are replaced tightly. If there are no bins, or if they are overflowing, carry all rubbish out with you. It is *not* a good policy to bury rubbish, as animals will dig it up later and scatter it around the camp.

- Develop a strict toilet policy, and explain it clearly to your clients. Some campers/caravanners/tour companies bring their own porta-potties on holiday. If so, only empty them at designated dump points as the chemicals can harm the environment.

- If you don't have a porta-potty, and the campsite has toilets (long-drops, biodegradable, flush type, whatever), get everyone to use them (even though sometimes they don't smell great!).

- If there are no toilets at a campsite, here's what we do. Take your loo roll, a small brown paper bag, and a designated spade to a private area that is not close to ponds, rivers, or other water supplies. Dig a small hole approximately 30–40 cm deep. Do your business and cover it well with dirt, then pat the area down with the spade. But do *not* bury the used toilet paper – animals will dig it up and scatter it all over the campsite. Instead, put the used toilet paper in the brown paper bag and bring it back to camp to a designated spot. Once most of the clients have gone to bed, Jeremy then burns all the bags in the campfire.

- Always keep a separate hand-washing basin about 1/3 full of water spiked with a few drops of Dettol to ensure personal hygiene for you and your clients.

- Tread lightly on the land. Organise a clean-up before you depart. Make the sure fire is completely out. Leave the campsite in better condition than you found it!

Set up a bush camp for safety and comfort, and know how to minimise the environmental impact. (Photo courtesy Global Gypsies.)

22

Basic Cooking and Hygiene

If you're providing bush catering for your clients, you need to enforce strict rules for cooking and hygiene.

In Western Australia, no licensing, legislative, or regulatory requirements apply at present to bush cooking, but these are sure to come. Whether or not you have regulations in your area, these guidelines may be of assistance:

- Menus should be nutritious, well balanced, varied, and appealing to the eye – don't serve up barbecued sausages or spaghetti bolognaise every night!
- Identify special dietary requirements/allergies in advance.
- Store food carefully, safely, hygienically, and at appropriate temperatures (consider refrigeration capabilities).
- Monitor food supplies throughout the tour to ensure freshness and adequate stocks.
- Check use-by dates carefully, and discard food that is past its expiry date.
- Dispose of leftover food safely and hygienically.
- Know which foods can be kept safely as leftovers – if in doubt, throw it out!
- Use clean utensils.

- Use at least two separate cutting boards – red for meat and green for vegetables (you can take this further if you wish using separate colours for cooked/uncooked meat, items which some clients may be allergic to, and so on).
- Check washing up carefully – use very hot water when you can.
- Keep kitchen tools, pots and pans, fridge, tabletops, stove, and all other catering equipment squeaky clean.
- Check water supply for safety and quantity – use only safe water for dishwashing if possible.
- Use latex gloves for food preparation.
- Keep hand-washing bowls handy, and spike them with disinfectant; encourage everyone to use them before touching or eating food.
- Use separate bowls for washing dishes, rinsing dishes, hand-washing, and body-washing.
- Limit access to the kitchen areas – don't allow clients to go into fridges, food preparation areas, or food supplies without prior permission. Ideally, the kitchen should be off limits to anyone except for the staff designated to prepare meals.
- Wash your personal set of crockery and cutlery separately – it's bad enough if clients pick up a bug, but you can't afford to!

On catered outback tours, companies usually tow a robust, specially designed, off-road catering trailer similar to this one. (Photo courtesy Global Gypsies.)

Bush catering doesn't have to be basic! Global Gypsies' al fresco Farewell Dinners with 1,000-star catering are affairs to remember! (Photo courtesy Global Gypsies.)

Tour Guide Tale #6: Bad Timing Equals Bad Trip

Because we're a small company we don't often employ other tour guides to lead our trips, but on this occasion we did. We'd worked out an itinerary, attracted the clients, made all the bookings for accommodation, national parks and attractions, and sub-contracted a guide with a good reputation to lead the week-long tour.

Looking back, we should have realised he had a timing problem – he was late for our initial discussions as well as a subsequent detailed briefing!

On the appointed day of the tour we were waiting at the departure point to farewell the group. The clients were all there, too, but where was the tour guide? Where was the coach? Half an hour late he turned up, and from there things went from bad to worse.

Our guide decided that the distances on the first day were too far to drive so, without our knowledge or approval, he stopped in a completely different town. This totally threw the itinerary off for the rest of the trip as he never made up the missed time. It also confused and angered the clients who had paid for a different itinerary, cost us money in cancellation fees at the caravan parks we had booked, and lost us credibility within the industry as we tried to explain the 'no-show' of our group to the various venue managers! We also still had to pay for the accommodation we had pre-booked!

Meals were served late, venue departures and arrivals were never on time and on one of the walks the group didn't get back till after dark – a huge 'no-no'. Although we managed to track the guide down several times during the tour, he never told us about these problems until the group returned and until we received a barrage of client complaints – our first ones ever!

From our perspective, the tour was a disaster. Wiser people than us have said 'timing is everything', and in this case that was certainly true. Needless to say we never used that tour guide again!

23

Cultural Issues

Whether you live in Australia, Canada, China, Japan, Kenya, New Zealand, South America, Thailand, UK, USA, or somewhere else, each destination has its own distinct cultural history and issues which are of great interest to visitors.

At our tour-guide training courses in Australia, we try to invite one or more indigenous participants to answer the many questions that clients ask us about Aboriginal issues when we take clients on tour. If no indigenous students are present, we open the subject up to the rest of the group for an informal discussion.

Imagine you're sitting around the campfire on our training course with a group of aspiring tour guides. What culturally related questions would you ask? What could you contribute to the discussion? Here are some of the topics we usually cover:

- How much do you know about the indigenous history of Australia? Of your own country?
- How much do you know about the colonial history of Australia? Of your country?

- Are there any particularly good books, documentaries, or TV shows that you'd recommend which increased your knowledge about cultural issues?
- Is it appropriate for non-indigenous tour guides to discuss indigenous culture and/or visit a country's sacred sites?
- If you do visit sacred sites without an indigenous guide, what information should you share with your clients? Who would you check with to ensure that your facts are correct and that you are exhibiting appropriate and culturally sensitive behaviour?
- How would you answer client questions about sensitive cultural issues in your country such as land rights, racism, the stolen generation, and illegal immigration? (Whatever your personal beliefs, as a tour guide, you should be objective and apolitical – remember that you are seen as an ambassador for your country. This isn't the time to get on your personal soapbox!)
- Have you (or has anyone in the group) experienced an indigenous tourism product? If so, what were your observations, comments, and memories?
- Have you attended any cultural forums or conferences? If so, what did you learn?
- You may have clients from overseas on your tours. Remember that their cultures may be completely different from yours – structure your presentation and behaviour accordingly, and be careful not to offend cultural sensitivities.
- When running a tour, try to include indigenous tourism experiences such as visiting a cultural venue, taking a tour with a local guide, or inviting a special guest speaker to address your group whenever possible.
- Bring plenty of reading material on cultural history and issues in your country. It's not only informative, but provides a factual, rather than emotional, basis for further discussions.

*There are a number of excellent indigenous tourism experiences available in
Australia. (Photo courtesy Tourism Western Australia/Captain Cook Cruises.)*

24

Interpretative and Narrative Skills

Okay, let's get our hands dirty! Let's talk about and get some practice with one of the most important aspects of tour guiding – interpretive and narrative skills. As a tour guide, an integral part of your role is to prepare and present interesting, factual commentary that your clients will understand, remember, and enjoy.

Here's how to master interpretation and narrative and put it to work for you:

A. Researching Your Narrative

Know your facts! Do your research and get the facts right! You can obtain information about your subject from the following sources:

- Your employer.
- The venue or attraction itself that you and your clients will be visiting.
- Local experts.
- Your own memory and experiences.
- Articles in newspapers or shows on TV.
- Internet (Wikipedia, Google, Yahoo).

- Phone apps (many of them are free).
- Libraries.
- Visitor centres.
- Travel manuals or directories.
- Reference or guide books.
- Word of mouth.
- Forums, seminars.
- Other tour guides.

B. Preparing Your Narrative

When preparing your narrative, follow this process:

Research ➡ *Understand* ➡ *Convey* ➡ *Engage*

- Write notes – but not a script. If you talk from a script or memorise your presentation word for word, you'll sound like a parrot! Best to use a breakdown of about 40 per cent script and 60 per cent personal delivery.
- Check your facts; ensure they are up to date.
- Know and like your topic.
- Seek expert advice or input on your topic when available.
- Make your presentation interesting and inspiring.
- Think how your presentation would come across if there is a language or disability barrier – you may need to make some adjustments.
- Write out your objectives – list the *three* most important points you want the audience to take away from your presentation, and build on it from there.
- Practice your presentation in front of the mirror or with friends or family.
- Don't just give your topic a name – give it a story!
- Get the right balance between generic and specific information – don't overload your listeners with too many boring statistics.

C. Training and Using Your Voice for Maximum Effect

- When delivering a presentation or narrative, your voice can be your greatest asset! Learn how to use it as a tool! Learn how to control volume, pitch, tone, inflection, and speed to change and improve your presentation and keep listeners interested.
- Project your voice! You do this from your stomach and diaphragm – not from your throat. Singers and stage actors know how to project their voices, even without a microphone. Strain your voice, and you'll get a sore throat or worse! Take a few singing or acting lessons, and you'll find that you'll start projecting your voice automatically.
- Learn how to use a microphone properly. Practice using the controls so you know how to adjust the volume, know the correct distance to hold the mike from your mouth, how to prevent squeal and feedback, and how to use a mike in a room and on a bus (quite different skills!).
- Practice delivering your presentation without a microphone in case it fails – which happens a lot! This is when your voice-projection techniques come in really handy!
- Protect your voice – smoking, yelling, and forcing your voice can cause temporary or even permanent damage.

D. Delivering Your Narrative

- On the day of your presentation, get up bright and early, and be well prepared.
- Consider such aspects as the age of the audience, their interests, the theme of your talk, and its relevance to your listeners – you may need to do some on-the-spot tweaking to suit the group.
- Keep it current; talk about what's there now. Nobody wants to hear, 'There used to be a beautiful old building here and,

over there, a lovely barn. What a pity they've been knocked down!'

- Tell your audience it's the *best ever* day to be doing your tour and one of the best you've ever run! They don't want to hear, 'You should have been here yesterday – we saw a huge mob of kangaroos and a massive pod of dolphins! Too bad there's nothing here today!'
- Be yourself! Don't copy somebody else's style. You aren't David Attenborough, Steve Irwin, or Bear Grylls – so don't try to be! Let the real you shine through!
- Be diplomatic, tactful, and politically correct.
- Try using props of some kind to punctuate your talk and add visual interest.
- Give your audience a chance to participate – involve and engage them! Ask them questions – *Who's been here before? Who's ever seen one of these? Does anyone know what this is?* and so on. Give them an activity to do, such as getting a volunteer involved in your presentation in a role play.
- Bring your interpretation to life.
- Tap into their emotions – people love a good love story, a hero, or a funny anecdote.
- Encourage your audience to touch/taste/feel/smell when possible and legally allowed – engage the senses! But remind your audience to take only photos home with them – no souvenirs (shells, plants, coral, rocks, etc.)
- Don't over-talk; sometimes, being quiet can be the best attention grabber of all.
- Leave your audience with a lasting impression and a take-home message.

Narrative is a crucial part of a tour guide's job. You need to inform, involve, and entertain your audience. (Photo courtesy Tourism Western Australia/Perth Mint.)

E. Evaluating Your Delivery

- After you've delivered your presentation, evaluate it.
- If circumstances permit, distribute a survey form to your audience, seeking feedback.
- Tape or video yourself during a routine presentation. Critique your performance – be tough and honest!
- Use the feedback to improve your delivery style and narrative content. Ask yourself, 'Would I enjoy this presentation? Would I relate to it? What would I take away from it?' If you think you need improvement, try changing your style and content, then practice and evaluate, practice and evaluate, until you're happy with the finished product.

If you're one of the thousands of people who are terrified of public speaking, you aren't alone! But here's some good advice – *get over it!*

To be an award-winning tour guide, delivering narrative will be a key part of your job.

The best way to get over your nerves, build your confidence, and improve your delivery style is to analyse what you find so frightening about public speaking, approach the situation rationally, work out some strategies, and *just keep practicing*. Some presenters find it helpful to pretend that they are speaking to just one person or to imagine that everyone in the audience is stark naked! But whatever tactics you employ, get your head around public speaking, and learn how to do it well.

25

The Art of Storytelling

A story is often the most memorable part of your commentary. Some people are natural-born storytellers, but if this particular skill doesn't come easily to you, here are some helpful hints:

- If you have a good imagination, create a story around the facts – but don't make the facts up. Authors do this all the time when they imagine what happened in the past as seen through a character's eyes – it's known as faction.
- Storytelling doesn't have to just be fictional or factional – it can include anecdotes, dreamtime stories, or biographies. The tale just has to be told in an interesting way to bring it to life.
- Introduce your story – paint the background picture first.
- Build the plot. This is when you can include facts and statistics, but not too many (!), and present them in an interesting way.
- Try using a bit of suspense and drama.
- Use visual props.
- Try using characterisation – take on the role and persona and speech patterns of someone in the tale.
- Don't leave long silences, but do allow for some quiet times – a pause can be perfect!
- Don't talk just for the sake of it. Keep the story sharp and crisp.

- Know how and when to end your story.
- Go out on a high! End your tale with a bang, not a whimper!

A. Storytelling Practice

Here are two ways you as the tour guide could tell the same story. After reading both versions, deliver the second approach yourself as if you were leading a real tour with real clients. Then choose some topics of your own, and have a few practice sessions.

Shipwreck in Busselton, Western Australia – Version 1

The Georgette *was a cargo and passenger ship wrecked off the Busselton coast in 1876.*

The Georgette *left Bunbury for Fremantle but developed a leak and started taking water. The crew couldn't get the pumps to work, and the boiler room became flooded. The decision was made to abandon ship, and the lifeboats were used, but twelve passengers drowned trying to reach the shore.*

The Georgette *drifted into the surf just a few kilometres north of where we are standing now. Fortunately, an Aboriginal stockman who worked for the Bussell family on their Margaret River property was watching from the cliffs. He returned to the homestead and raised the alarm.*

Young Grace Bussell who lived in the homestead was just sixteen years old. She departed on horseback and rode down a steep cliff to the beach and into the sea. Thanks to her heroic efforts, the Aboriginal stockman, and several other local families who provided assistance, fifty people were saved.

Grace's legend lives on through the name of the coastal hamlet of Gracetown, north of Margaret River, and the wheatbelt town of Lake Grace.

Did you enjoy this story? Or did you find it a bit dull? To tell it with a bit more life and colour and to keep your audience enthralled, try this version:

Shipwreck in Busselton, Western Australia – Version 2

I'd like to tell you a story about a lady who I call Amazing Grace. Sixteen-year-old Grace Bussell is one of WA's heroes, and the events that made her famous over 150 years ago happened right here on this very beach (pause for effect).

In 1876, the Georgette, *a ship powered by sail and steam, left the port of Bunbury, headed for Fremantle. She was carrying passengers and a heavy cargo of jarrah wood. Not long into her journey – straight out that way about 15 km (point in appropriate direction) and in the dark of night – she started taking water.*

Unbeknownst to the hapless crew and passengers, the bilge pump was faulty, and some say the ship was overloaded and in need of repair. Water started pouring into the engine room, but the pump couldn't cope – it was ankle-deep and rising. The sailors did their best, but by daybreak, the boiler room was awash, the coal fires running the engine had been swamped, and the Georgette *was adrift in a rising swell.*

Somehow, the ship battled its way to within fifty metres of the rugged shore, but the waves were three metres high with rips and swells. The captain yelled, 'Abandon ship!' Lifeboats were swung over the side. Imagine the terror of the passengers amidst the panic and chaos! Hear the roar of the crashing waves, the shouts of the crew, the screams of the women, and the creaking of the ship as she began to break up!

Several passengers were bundled into a lifeboat, but as it was being lowered, it smashed into the hull of the mother ship. Crash! The lifeboat tipped over, and its occupants were thrown into the sea. Some were drowned. The crew helped the rest of the passengers battle their way to the beach in other lifeboats; some attempted to swim.

Four crewmen reached the shore where they secured a small boat with heavy cables. They used the cable as a lifeline to steady the other lifeboats crowded with passengers as they were pulled into shore, a daunting task which took numerous journeys over several hours.

Meanwhile, an Aboriginal stockman named Sam Isaacs was riding home from a nearby dairy along the cliff just above us. Sam worked for Alfred and Ellen Bussell and their young family, one of WA's famous farming dynasties, at their property Wallcliffe. Suddenly, he saw the broken ship, the bobbing lifeboats, and the people struggling in the ocean. Shipwreck! He raced his horse to the homestead, completing the 15-km journey in record time.

Only Grace and her mother were there but knew they had to help. Ellen said she'd open her house to the survivors. Grace, who was a bit of a tomboy and an accomplished horsewoman with the heart of a lion, grabbed some ropes, leaped onto her horse, and galloped back to the cliff with Sam Isaacs.

The narrow track leading down to the beach was steep and treacherous. Onlookers said later that it seemed impossible that Sam and Grace could make it down the slope at such a pace, but make it they did. They stormed on to the beach, riding straight into the roaring surf to reach the lifeboats and struggling swimmers. At one point, Grace's horse stumbled in the churning water, and she almost fell off, but she managed to regain her mount and continue with the rescue.

Several women and children grabbed tightly on to the ropes she'd brought with her, and Grace and Sam courageously began helping survivors on to shore. Meanwhile, several other townsfolk had arrived to help. Well-known families like the MacGregors, Harwoods, Scotts, Yelvertons, Abbeys, Guerriers, and Brockmans all came to assist and later returned to provide provisions and dry clothes.

A total of twelve people died on that tragic night, but many more would have drowned had it not been for brave young Grace Bussell, Sam Isaacs, and the neighbouring families. Newspapers around the world picked up the story, and all the rescuers were hailed as heroes, but even in those days, the media loved the angle of a gutsy young woman saving the day so tended to give Grace most of the attention. As a result, she got stacks of fan mail along with marriage proposals from around the world from men she'd never met!

Sam and Grace were awarded medals by the Royal Humane Society for their bravery, while Gracetown, just north of here, and the wheatbelt town of Lake Grace were both named after young Grace Bussell. Here's a photo of her that I carry with me. She was one incredible lady, all right – our very own Amazing Grace.

For variation, you could tell the story from a child's point of view who survived the shipwreck or from Sam Isaac's perspective or even from the horse's mouth!

You might be thinking, 'Well, it's easy to tell a good story about an adventure like that, but what about a more mundane topic, such as a building?' Here's an example of how you can tell a 'tamer' story in two different ways:

A Visit to Inn Mahogany Creek – Version 1

The inn at Mahogany Creek is a well-known West-Australian landmark. Originally named The Prince of Wales Inn, it was built on a spacious 3.5-acre block from local stone in the mid 1800s.

Established by the businesswoman Jane Byfield, The Prince of Wales was a simple yet homey wayside inn where weary travellers could rest and dine. Known today as Inn Mahogany Creek, this beautiful Georgian building still stands and is one of Perth's oldest operating inns.

With high-profile owners such as Sir Stephen Parker, a prominent politician and Chief Justice of the Supreme Court of WA, the inn has had a varied and exciting history – from being used as a bushrangers hideout, to possibly being haunted, to being the inn where the notorious criminal and Australian cultural icon Moondyne Joe was reportedly captured after years on the run . . .

Find this a teensy bit boring? Try this version:

A Visit to Inn Mahogany Creek – Version 2

Imagine you're living in Western Australia in the 1850s. It would have been a wild and woolly place in those days. Convicts were arriving thick and fast, and WA was experiencing a period of rapid growth and change.

This lovely old inn is situated about halfway between York and Perth. York is the oldest inland town in the state, and many people arriving in WA headed there on horseback, in carriages, or on foot to start a new life. They would have stopped here, possibly where we are standing right now, to water their horses, spend the night, or have a meal. They may have even seen some bushrangers; it's said they used the inn as a hideout.

Today, we know this place as Inn Mahogany Creek, but back then it was called the Prince of Wales. It was built on a spacious 3.5-acre block from local stone in the mid 1800s by a successful businesswoman named Jane Byfield. Later renamed after the nearby Mahogany Creek, this beautiful Georgian building is one of Perth's oldest operating inns.

Some folks say it's haunted by the ghost of WA's most famous bushranger, Moondyne Joe. He was reportedly once captured here after years on the run – one of his many captures and escapes!

Moondyne Joe was no Ned Kelly; he mainly stole livestock rather than holding up stagecoaches, but he was a clever and elusive character who spent a lot of time getting in and breaking out of jail! He remains one of the most romantic and legendary figures in our state's history.

In recent years, the inn has become more sedate with high-profile owners such as Sir Stephen Parker, a prominent politician and Chief Justice of the Supreme Court of WA. Nowadays, it's a favourite spot for tourists visiting the Perth hills or the Avon Valley to enjoy a meal or afternoon tea.

But I like to think of it as it was in the old days. As we walk around the grounds, keep your eyes open for the ghost of Moondyne Joe or for some other dodgy bushrangers. You never know when they might pop up to give you a scare!

For variation, tell the story from Moondyne Joe's point of view or through the eyes of one of the pastoralists or even from the viewpoint of a mature tree in the garden that has witnessed history unfold from the time the inn was first built. By using your imagination, there are infinite ways that you can tell a story that is factual but which also entertains your audience and retains their interest.

Tour Guide Tale #7: Rescue in the Grand Canyon

Long before Global Gypsies existed, Jan went on a private trip to the Grand Canyon. She had booked on the famous mule ride from the canyon rim down to Phantom Ranch where you stay overnight in the bunkhouse, then ride back up to the rim the next day. The Grand Canyon is 446 km (277 miles) long, 29 km (18 miles) wide, and over 1,800 m deep (that's 6,000 feet or more than a scary vertical mile straight down!). For someone with less-than-average equine skills, venturing down there on a mule was already an exciting and nail-biting prospect, but it turned out to be even more adventurous than expected!

The mule trail is narrow, winding, and rocky. At times, it feels as if your whole body is leaning over into the deep crevasse almost a mile below. You find yourself holding on to the bridle with white knuckles and clinging on to the saddle with thigh muscles you never knew you had! Sometimes, you find yourself holding your breath from sheer terror, but it's so exhilarating that you savour every minute. You don't have to be a good rider (though it probably helps!), but you definitely need to have complete faith in your sure-footed mule and in your expert cowboy (or cowgirl in this case) tour guide.

Before departing, clients are given an extensive safety briefing and asked to sign a lengthy disclaimer. In that document, they advise you not to go on the tour if you suffer from vertigo, are afraid of mules or horses, if you've never ridden before, or if you have a heart condition.

Jan's small group began the descent on their trusty mules – the scenery was magnificent, and she was loving the experience. But when they stopped for lunch a couple of hours later, one of the women on the tour began having a panic attack. She was so terrified that she refused to get off her mule. The tour guide tried to help her dismount, but the client was shaking so much that she fell off, landed awkwardly, and broke her ankle as she hit the ground. Disaster! The group was too far down to go back up and too far from the bottom to continue down to the homestead.

As a trained first-aider, the tour guide said the only option was to call for a rescue helicopter and have the woman evacuated to the closest hospital on the canyon rim. She handled the situation brilliantly, making sure that everyone was OK while she tended to the injured client and called for the heli on a strategically placed emergency phone.

In no time, a rescue heli was whirring its way down the canyon, medics had loaded the injured woman on board, and the heli was making its way skywards. For Jan, it was a fascinating experience to see such an exciting real-life emergency and to observe how expertly it had been handled. For the tour guide, it must have been a nightmare; although apparently, it was not the first time she had dealt with such an emergency.

It later transpired that the client had not been truthful when she signed her disclaimer. Not only did she suffer from vertigo and dizziness, she was also petrified of horses and mules, had never been horse-riding in her life, *and* was taking medication for a heart condition. She should never have been on this tour in the first place but was participating because she had allowed her pushy husband to talk her into it.

As a tour guide, there's a saddlebag of lessons you can take away from this incident. Lesson 1 would be to check client-disclaimer forms carefully and request a medical certificate if you have doubts about the veracity of what's been included. Lesson 2 would be to ensure that all clients are *willing* participants in an activity, particularly if it involves risk. Lesson 3 would be that even if, in spite of your best efforts, things turn ugly, be sure you know what to do in case of an emergency. Can you think of additional lessons that can be learned from this experience?

As an aside, since we set up Global Gypsies, we've had several clients tell fibs on their disclaimer forms about the state of their health so that they can join the tour. When we've had concerns, we've insisted on a medical certificate. In some cases, we've had to say 'Sorry, but for safety reasons, you can't come.' Sometimes, tough love is the best kind!

When visiting the USA's Grand Canyon, the optional two-day mule ride between the rim and the canyon floor is a popular activity for many visitors, but it can also be challenging. (Photo courtesy Global Gypsies.)

26

Walk the Walk: A Role Play

Okay, let's get some more practice! On our tour-guide training course, we take the students out for a bush walk, and everyone gets a chance to be the leader. While they're leading the tour and doing their best to deliver an interesting and informative narrative, we're creating all kinds of diversionary and disruptive chaos behind the scenes, which the tour guide has to deal with while still keeping the tour on track.

The role play sounds like, and is, a lot of fun, but it's also great practice. As we can't do this with you in person, to test your skills, pretend you are the tour leader of a group of clients on a walk in the bush, in the forest, or somewhere else outdoors, or even in an indoor museum or art gallery. Think about how you would cope in the following situations. These scenarios have all actually happened, and you'll probably need to deal with them one day!

Before you read the recommended action to take, first consider what your response would be in a real-life situation. No peeking or reading ahead!

Scenario 1:

You've done your headcount before you set out, but fifteen minutes into your tour, you realise someone is missing from your group.

Solution:

In this role play, we deliberately asked someone to disappear from the walk to emphasise the importance of doing regular headcounts. In a real-life situation, you should have everyone else stay in one place while you go back and try to find the missing person. If you can't find them in a few minutes, you may need to implement an emergency plan, but be careful that you don't lose other group members in the process.

This situation can be prevented by conducting regular headcounts throughout your tour, by giving clear instructions at the outset of your walk, by allocating everyone 'buddies' or walking partners, or by appointing a 'tail-end Charlie' to ensure the group stays together and there are no stragglers.

Scenario 2:

An argument breaks out between two clients, possibly a couple having a 'domestic', which is interrupting your presentation and disturbing the other clients. How do you calm the two people down and continue to deliver your tour to the rest of the group?

Solution:

Approach the arguing clients privately, and try to help them to resolve the matter. If you have no luck, ask them to press the pause button until your tour is over as they are disrupting the enjoyment of the other clients. As a last resort, ask them to leave the tour and continue their lively discussion somewhere else.

Scenario 3:

Some of the clients keep wandering off to take photos, check out plants, and generally just do their own thing.

Solution:

This situation often occurs when clients have a particular interest in a topic, want to get a closer look, or take a photo. Heaven forbid it's because they're bored with your presentation!

You can help prevent it happening by giving clear instructions at the outset of your walk about the need to stay together, allocating buddies or walking partners, building photo opportunities into the tour, and by actively involving the wanderers in your presentation.

If you do get wanderers, politely ask them to stay with the group. Tell them they will be missing important information, could become lost, and that they are compromising your duty of care as you are responsible for their welfare while they are on your tour.

Scenario 4:

An international visitor who speaks little or no English can't understand your presentation.

Solution:

Try to include more visual explanations in your presentation, use props, try to physically involve the person in the activity. And if you have an iPhone, use the foreign-language dictionary or interpretive app to translate keywords. Show them pictures in reference books or on iPhone apps.

Scenario 5:

A client takes a souvenir, picks a flower, or feeds a wild animal.

Solution:

This can be prevented by clearly explaining the Leave No Trace principles in your initial welcome remarks. If someone ignores your instructions, stop the tour and explain the principles again. Usually, once you educate the client as to why we don't take souvenirs, the problem should go away.

Scenario 6:

A know-it-all client keeps contradicting your comments or interrupting your talk with interesting facts of their own.

Solution:

Thank the client for his/her comments. Say something like, 'You obviously have a lot of knowledge about this topic. We're really enjoying your contributions, but we need to keep to the schedule. I'd love to have a chat with you privately about this subject after the tour to learn more. Can we catch up later to discuss it in more depth?'

Scenario 7:

A client flirts openly with you in front of the group.

Solution:

Flirting can be flattering, but it can also be very awkward and potentially embarrassing when you are trying to lead a group tour. You can help prevent this situation by talking about your partner (real or imaginary) in your opening remarks, by wearing a wedding ring, and by not playing favourites.

If the attention becomes uncomfortable, and your gentle hints aren't working, you may need to take the person aside privately. Explain that you're flattered but unavailable and that their attention is making you feel embarrassed and is affecting group dynamics and the enjoyment of the tour for other clients.

If you're keen to pursue the relationship, do so discreetly after the tour has finished – but not during it!

Scenario 8:

Someone trips over and hurts themselves.

Solution:

This is when your first-aid training and the first-aid kit that you always carry in your backpack come in handy! Depending on the severity of the injury, your training will dictate how to deal with it and what should happen next. If the situation is not too serious, ask the group to wait in a designated spot while you attend to the injured client. Make sure they all stick together – you may want to appoint someone to be a 'shepherd' while you tend to the injury. There are no hard and fast rules here; you'll need to deal with each situation individually depending on the specific circumstances. But general guidelines are to think clearly, stay calm, be proficient in first-aid, and know how to deal with emergencies.

Scenario 9:

A client faints.

Solution:

Dehydration is a very common occurrence on tour and often causes clients to faint. Dehydration can be due to people doing more exercise than normal, not drinking enough to compensate for the extra activity, and being outside in warmer conditions than they may be accustomed to.

If a client is suffering from dehydration, give them a drink of room-temperature (not cold) water, sit them down in a cool place, and let them rest. We usually follow this up with a dose of an electrolyte supplement such as Aqualyte – we go through heaps of it on our tours – and then monitor the client for twenty-four hours.

However, if you think the fainting is caused by something more serious than dehydration, rely on your first-aid training to tell you what else to check for and what action to take.

Scenario 10:

A client suffers a heart attack, severe allergic reaction, or other life-threatening medical emergency while on tour.

Solution:

Go into emergency mode. Follow the rules you've learnt at your first-aid course. Get someone to call an ambulance or other rescue service on their mobile (or on the sat phone you always carry with you if you are out of mobile range) – dial 000 or 112. Appoint a shepherd to keep the group together while you look after the casualty, and go through your established first-aid and emergency procedures.

27

How to Lead Different Types of Tours

There are a number of different types of tours. The best way to learn how to lead them properly is to see the professionals at work. Check with your local tourism authority to find out who the best operators are in your area – then go on a tour with them as a client. Be objective, enjoy the experience, take notes, watch, and learn! Show enough enthusiasm, and you may even end up with a job with them one day!

A. Short Tours on Foot

In most cities and surrounds, there are numerous guided tours available with varied themes. In Perth and Fremantle, for example, there are tours of Parliament House, Fremantle Prison, Perth Mint, museums, Kings Park, Swan Bells, and other iconic venues. There are also operators offering indigenous tours or tours that focus on wine, food, shopping, history, and more. Here are the basic rules for leading a short tour, most of which apply to other types of tours as well:

- Be familiar with the timing and frequency of the tours.
- Know your subject.
- Know the route.
- Stick to your timetable.

- Introduce yourself to the group before you begin your presentation.
- Know how to project your voice.
- When delivering your presentation, position yourself for best effect (consider angle of sun, their ability to hear and see you, access to shade or seating for clients, and views of the attraction from *their* perspective).
- Know (or develop) the policy on minimum/maximum group size.
- Arrange stopping points in advance.
- Learn how to master walking and talking – don't do both at the same time! Stop walking, face your audience, make sure you have everyone's attention, and *then* start talking.
- Leave time in your presentation for questions, and let clients know when you want to answer them (during or after your talk?).
- Be familiar with possible risks and occupational health and safety requirements.
- Be proud of your personal appearance (clean uniform, visible name badge, appropriate footwear).
- Tailor your presentation and narrative for each group.
- Consider how you will deal with groups (or individuals) with special needs and/or disabilities, and tailor your presentation (and possibly your tour route) accordingly.
- Speak S-L-O-W-L-Y and clearly. Don't' be a marble mouth! And don't use slang. International travellers won't understand what you're saying!
- Remember to distribute flyers, brochures, and survey forms (if any).
- Have clients sign any relevant disclaimer forms before starting their tour.
- This may sound repetitive, but do regular headcounts – *before, during, and after your tour!*
- Keep the group together (experiment with various techniques such as having them walk single-file, walk with a buddy, or

initiate some group interaction, make regular stops to deliver commentary, and so on).

- Set the pace depending on the group.
- Have (or develop) a theme for your presentation.
- Practice techniques to stay in control and hold the group's attention (change the pitch, tone, or level of your voice; do something unexpected; go silent for a while; ask your group to be completely silent to listen to a bird, waterfall, or something similar; clap, whistle, sing, or laugh during your presentation – but make sure you feel comfortable doing your attention-grabbing trick!)
- Continue to learn about your subject and build on your knowledge base.
- Integrate your knowledge with that of your fellow guides.
- Maintain your enthusiasm.
- To avoid embarrassing and awkward moments, know (or develop) the policy on tipping (for yourself, the driver, porters, etc.).

Visitors enjoy a guided tour through the tunnels of historic Fremantle Prison. (Photo courtesy Tourism Western Australia/Fremantle Prison.)

B. Meet-and-Greets and Client Departures

Many guides are asked to do meet-and-greets (welcoming clients on arrival at airports, train or bus stations, or ports) or to assist clients with departures. Here's a checklist to use on these occasions:

- Check and double check client names, arrival/departure details, last-minute flight/train schedule changes.
- Be familiar with group check-in procedures at airports and train or bus stations.
- Liaise in advance with coach drivers who will be transporting clients to/from airport/station.
- Arrange how you will get to airport/station and home again.
- Arrive early.
- Be mindful of your personal appearance.
- Prepare clear, legible signage for arriving clients (size, legibility, spelling).
- Check that outgoing clients have passports and other documents before leaving the hotel.
- Always position yourself in the airport/station so clients can see you.
- Be familiar with airport/train-station security/access.
- Work with the tour leader (if there is one).
- Oversee loading of coach, and check number of pieces of luggage.
- Give positive, informative commentary about your city en route to the hotel or other destination.
- Be aware that clients who have been on a long flight may be tired – try not to overload them with too much information or complicated instructions.
- Make advance contact with the hotel re: check-in/check-out times.
- Make a list of handy things to carry with you (pen, paper, phone, charger, maps, etc.).
- Ensure outgoing clients have all necessary documentation and have completed appropriate departure cards.
- Know (or develop) the policy on tipping.

C. Short Tours in Vehicles

On these tours, you may be working with a driver, or you may be working alone. In addition to the points listed in A, the following guidelines apply to both drivers and guides when leading tours in which clients are travelling as passengers in your vehicle:

- Be early.
- Dress for the occasion (uniform, name badge, hat, appropriate shoes).
- Familiarise yourself with your equipment and the vehicle.
- Complete necessary paperwork before leaving depot.
- Coordinate various pick-ups in advance.
- Be familiar with tour route and timing.
- Build a rapport with your suppliers (managers of venues, accommodation, restaurants, attractions you'll be visiting, etc.).
- Give each client a warm welcome.
- Establish a rapport with your passengers from the outset – introduce yourself, smile!
- Discuss the basic format and itinerary of the tour *before* you leave to ensure all the clients are on the right tour and on the right coach.
- Distribute relevant flyers and brochures about the tour.
- Explain any safety procedures.
- Assist passengers on/off vehicle.
- Be safety conscious when dropping clients off (traffic hazards, curbs, etc.).
- Arrange timely comfort stops, ideally to coincide with other activities, such as visiting points of interest).
- When making stops, provide adequate time to disembark, visit destination, re-embark – it takes longer to shepherd a group than to work with just one or two people.
- Give very clear instructions as to departure times and where to meet, and make sure everyone understands them (particularly international visitors). It's best to state departure times *two*

different ways just to be certain! For example, 'We leave here at 2.30,' or 'We have thirty minutes here, it is now two o'clock, so you need to be back in half an hour.'

- Here it is again – do headcounts!
- Know and practice your commentary.
- Know how the public-address system/microphone works and use it (if there is one).
- Make your comments relevant and interesting.
- Use appropriate language – keep it simple.
- Distribute survey/feedback forms (if any) in time for clients to return them before the trip ends.
- Check vehicle for client possessions before returning to the depot.
- Complete paperwork before going home.
- Leave vehicle clean and tidy.

Medium-sized buses designed to stay on tarred roads are often used to transport clients taking guided tours. (Photo courtesy Global Gypsies/Western Travel Bug.)

D. Extended Tours in Coaches or 4WD Vehicles

On extended tours, clients may be passengers in coaches travelling on surfaced roads or in 4WD vehicles travelling on outback roads and tracks. Whichever type of tour you're leading, you'll need to apply everything you've learnt previously and then some! Here are our suggestions, many of which also apply to tag-along tours in which clients drive their own 4×4 vehicles and travel in a convoy led by an expert guide, such as those run by Global Gypsies:

1. Think about Yourself!

- Be prepared for long days and long hours of driving.
- Some budget-style companies only use one driver/guide. Hopefully, your company will employ two people per tour, either two drivers/guides or a driver/guide assisted by a cook or hostess, but be prepared for the possibility that you may be working on your own.
- You'll be away from home a lot – you need to have a supportive and understanding partner and/or family.
- Things don't always go according to plan. Be flexible/improvisational; have a Plan B.
- Pace yourself; don't run yourself into the ground.
- Prepare well for your tour.
- Be organised – make sure everything has its proper place and stays there.
- Keep a diary or notebook to record events (bullet points are fine).
- Remember that you're always on show – your clients don't miss a trick!
- Respect and work together with service providers and other operators.
- Leave your personal problems at home.
- Pack smart – too much gear, no idea!

- Do your homework – there will be hundreds of facts about numerous places for you to remember and include in your commentary.
- Bring reference books, magazines, and articles to jog your own memory and for the benefit of the clients who want to read up on certain topics during those long hours on the road.
- Don't take unnecessary risks.
- Keep your first-aid certificate current – we guarantee you'll need it at least once on an   extended tour!
- Lead by example.
- Be a credible and consistent leader – the longer the tour, the more important this becomes!
- Maintain your enthusiasm (particularly towards the end of the tour).
- Keep healthy, eat well, limit alcohol, and get plenty of sleep (when you can!).

2. Of Particular Importance on Longer Tours

- Occupational health and safety concerns.
- Knowing how to deal with difficult clients – the longer the tour, the greater the likelihood of having tough customers.
- Be constantly aware of group dynamics, cultural sensitivities, and special needs.
- Personal appearance – comfort vs professionalism. You need to find a middle ground.
- Stick to the itinerary – on a longer tour, once you get behind, you'll never catch up!
- Establish regular meal times for you and the group.
- Get clients to help you with tasks if you wish. We use a client roster, and it works a treat!
- Rotate client seating positions – no nesting or favourite seats.
- Try to be early to bed, early to rise.
- Know how to deal with emergencies.
- Write reports, including incident reports, promptly.

A guided bush walk through Purnululu National Park (Bungle Bungles) is one of the highlights of WA's Kimberley region. (Photo courtesy Global Gypsies.)

3. Get to Know Your Clients

- Try to learn about your clients before the tour begins – ask your employer to show you the client-booking forms or give you a briefing about the people on your tour.
- Find out *before* you depart if anyone in the group has any special dietary requirements or food allergies. Are there vegetarians, vegans, coeliacs, diabetics, those who need gluten-free or lactose-free foods, etc.? It's likely that someone on your tour does require special food, so make sure that you've catered for them appropriately. Your company should have this information recorded on their booking forms and made appropriate catering arrangements, but sometimes, this information slips through the net. This means you have a huge problem once you're on the road; whereas if you find out early, you'll still have time to hit the shops before you leave.

- Have a get-to-know-you session on the first night – ask everyone to introduce themselves and tell the group a little about themselves, why they're on the tour, and so on.
- Understand the customer profile your company is targeting. Is it backpackers? Luxury travellers? Baby boomers? Eco-tourists? Adventure seekers? Solo travellers? Special-interest groups? Children? Students? Domestic travellers, international travellers, or a combination of all the above? Adjust your content and delivery style accordingly.
- Once you get to know your group, you may need to adjust your presentations and activities even further. For example, are they first-time or experienced travellers? History, plant, or animal buffs? Independent or needy? Keen photographers? Helpful? Lazy? Fit? Fragile? Young? Old? Or are they party people who don't care where they are as long as there's beer? At some point, you'll have *every* type under the sun!
- Some individuals and client types will be more interested and receptive to the content of your presentations than others. Try not to get disheartened if some people don't seem that interested; others in the group may be riveted and will be disappointed if you stop delivering!
- If a large number of your company's clients seem to come from particular destinations, learn a bit about their home countries.
- Even though international clients may speak English, it may be their second or third language. Speak slowly and clearly and avoid slang and sarcasm.
- If you have older clients, consider such issues as mobility, stairs, or steps, the difficulty they have with sleeping on the ground when camping, the possibility of disorientation, use of medication, frequent toilet stops, preference for regular meal times, early nights, need for softer itineraries, etc.
- Know how to deal with couples (don't show preference for the partner of the opposite sex!).
- Know how to deal with singles (don't let your attention be misconstrued as flirting).

- Don't play favourites – try to give each client the same amount of attention.
- Be prepared to put on your problem-solver hat – on longer tours, you'll have more problems to deal with than on shorter tours.

On camping adventures, clients usually sleep in tents provided by the tour operator. (Photo courtesy Coates Wildlife Tours.)

4. Equipment

On extended tours which include camping or catering, in addition to your personal gear, you may need to take such equipment as:

- Tents.
- Mattresses or swags.
- Stretchers.
- Crockery and cutlery.
- Tarpaulins.
- Jerry cans.
- First-aid equipment.
- Food.
- Water.
- Luggage or catering trailer.

- Tables and chairs.
- Toolbox.
- Spare parts.
- Vehicle-recovery gear.
- Emergency communications gear – and more!

Remember that clients may not know how to use tour equipment correctly or look after it properly. Explain to them on Day 1 which gear they can handle and which gear they can't and show them how to use it correctly. Then keep a watchful eye on equipment and supplies – replacing things can be difficult and expensive, or often impossible, once you're away from your base.

On catered tours, explain to clients the importance of stringent kitchen hygiene – you don't want germs to spread throughout the group. Also, keep tight control of food and water so you don't run out of supplies, and show clients how to correctly use, clean, and maintain catering equipment. See Chapter 22 for more details on bush cooking.

5. Basic Mechanical Skills and Vehicle Maintenance

On extended tours, we recommend that drivers and/or guides conduct the following *daily* vehicular checks – if done correctly, they should prevent major mechanical problems from occurring. It's a good idea to conduct this check at the *end* of each day when there is more time to fix any problems before the next day's driving. An abbreviated check should also be carried out before driving the next morning. Specific items to check will vary between vehicles but should typically include:

- Tyres: pressures, cuts and chips.
- Suspension and chassis: no leaks from shocks, no cracks in chassis.
- Underbody: general check for fluids, leaks, splashing, and anything loose, bent, or damaged; remember to check the exhaust pipe.

- External: general check and after-market gear, e.g., roof rack, antenna, spare-wheel carrier, long range fuel tank, etc.
- Lights: brake, indicators, emergency, also lights on luggage or catering trailer.
- Under bonnet: check for loose hoses, belts, fluid loss, loose components.
- Fluids: oils, coolant, and brake and power-steering fluid.
- Battery: check that it is secure, especially nuts and bolts holding bracket and terminals secure, top-up cells if necessary.
- Radiator: reasonably clean and free of grass seeds, bugs, mud, etc.
- Air filter: check and clean.
- Visibility: windscreen-washer fluid, no cracks, all lights working (including lights on luggage or catering trailer).
- Internal: ensure cargo system is secure, fire extinguisher and first-aid kit are in place, instruments are working correctly; check fuel level.

If you're venturing into remote areas or will be doing any four-wheel driving, we recommend that, as a *minimum*, you take a basic mechanical course and a 4WD-training course before heading out with a group of clients. Taking clients on an extended tour is a huge responsibility – their lives are literally in your hands!

The Australian Outback is incredible, but it is also challenging and unforgiving. Tour guides taking clients into remote areas need to have special skills, experience, and equipment. (Photo courtesy Global Gypsies.)

6. Basic Bush-Survival Skills

If you're leading tours in remote areas, you need to know some basic bush-survival skills. We won't go into this subject in detail here; to gain more knowledge, either do some extra reading or take a hands-on training course (for example, the City Slicker to Outback Jack weekend course developed by Global Gypsies which covers basic bush mechanics, basic bush-survival skills, remote-area travel planning, and introductory 4WD'ing and towing).

But in summary, when leading a tour to the outback or any remote area, the most important things to remember are:

- Have a plan so you know what to do in case something goes wrong (vehicle breakdown, getting lost, emergency, stranded due to extreme weather conditions or natural disaster).
- Take some emergency water and rations.
- Carry a first-aid kit and thermal blankets, and know how to use them.
- Carry an EPIRB or sat phone and charger, and know how to use them.
- Make sure that the relevant people (your company, local authorities, or police) know where you're going and when you're expected back.

If there is an accident or emergency:

- Deal with any injuries first.
- Implement your emergency plan.
- Stay with the vehicle – don't walk away to seek help.
- Keep the group together; don't allow anyone to wander off.
- Conserve water and supplies.
- Stay sheltered and out of the elements.
- Conserve everyone's energy.
- Make signals to attract attention – SOS on the ground in stones or a small smoky fire.
- Know how to find water (human beings can only survive hours without water but several days without food).
- Stay in control of the group – be a strong leader, make rules, allocate duties, and implement your emergency plan.

Tour Guide Tale #8: Emergency Outback Rescue

Jeremy was once leading a tour for another company in a remote and rugged area of North West Australia. The tour involved quite a strenuous walk in temperatures of over 40°C (100°F); participants needed to be quite fit to attempt it.

At a client briefing before the walk, Jeremy told the clients that they *must* be in a good state of health in order to participate. He emphasised that they must be able to climb up and make sharp descents over large rocks and boulders and be able to walk for extended periods in the heat.

One European woman was not an ideal candidate to participate; she was overweight, not used to walking, and a smoker. Jeremy counselled her not to go on the walk as diplomatically as possible. When she refused to take his advice, he became more forceful, pointing out the risks involved and addressing her lack of physical fitness. He was careful to ensure that other clients witnessed the discussion and were aware of his concerns.

When the woman still insisted that she should go on the walk and refused to heed his warnings, Jeremy approached her husband, hoping that he would convince the woman not to participate. But the husband also insisted that she should go, so against all sensible and informed advice, off they went.

Several hours later, the woman completed the walk but with difficulty. She returned to camp completely exhausted and went straight to her tent. Jeremy checked on her; she said she was fine, just tired. But this story doesn't have a happy ending.

The woman awoke the next morning feeling dizzy and unwell; worst of all, her face was half paralysed. Jeremy followed the company's emergency procedures, went into first-aid mode, and, after checking and recording her symptoms, diagnosed a stroke. He phoned the Royal Flying Doctor Service (RFDS) on his satellite phone, requesting an urgent evacuation.

The RFDS agreed with his diagnosis and immediately dispatched a rescue plane to fly her to the nearest regional hospital. Unfortunately, the woman's symptoms worsened during the flight, and the medics decided to fly her to the intensive-care unit of a major hospital in Perth. After several weeks of treatment, she was flown back to Europe, where it took her several months to recover.

This incident raises the ethical question of just how forceful a guide can be when telling a client that they shouldn't participate in an activity for health or safety reasons. And if they refuse to listen, how does the guide physically prevent them from participating? It's a hard call and one that you may be faced with someday. Think about what you would do if faced with a similar dilemma.

In hindsight, Jeremy thinks that he handled the incident as best as he could with his level of experience and maturity at the time. However, today he would be much tougher. One option he might use is to threaten to cancel the walk altogether. It is then likely that peer-group pressure would resolve the situation.

But his favourite solution is to make all the clients climb from the ground right over the top of his vehicle and down the other side before they tackle a challenging walk. That determines their level of fitness and agility and lets them see for themselves if they're up to it. If they can't climb the cruiser, they can't take the walk!

40 Golden Rules of Travelling in the Outback

Here's a list of rules we give to our clients who, after joining us on a 4WD convoy tour, may travel to remote areas in the future independently. Feel free to use the list for your own personal purposes!

- Never travel alone. Go with friends, a club, or a professional tag-along tour operator.
- Don't go off the bitumen with a 2WD vehicle or with a caravan, camper, or any other vehicle that is not specifically designed for challenging off-road travel.
- Tell a friend or family member where you're going and when you're expected back.
- Let the police in the area know your travel plans – and remember to check in with them when you get back safely so they don't send out a search party!
- Plan ahead – be well equipped.
- Know the capabilities of you and your vehicle.
- Have some practice runs first – join a 4WD or caravan club and test your equipment, your knowledge, and your ability to deal with problems.
- Keep your 4WD vehicle well maintained.
- Carry extra spare parts for your vehicle and your caravan/camper trailer.
- Plan your route carefully, taking into consideration such important aspects as road conditions, weather forecasts, overnight stops, fuel stops, availability of food, water, etc.
- Carry detailed maps and/or a GPS, and know how to use them.
- Carry an Electronic Position Indicating Radio Beacon – EPIRB for short – for life-threatening emergencies, and know how to use it.
- Install a vehicle-mounted UHF two-way radio and learn how to use it (this only has sufficient range to communicate between vehicles travelling in close proximity).

- Consider installing an HF radio and joining the HFoZ radio network.
- Carry a satellite phone – know how to use it, and make sure it's charged (mobile phones will not have reception in remote areas).
- Don't take unnecessary risks – check out unfamiliar tracks or river crossings first, either by walking them or by asking other travellers you may meet on the road or via two-way radio.
- Carry extra water and moist tinned food.
- Make sure you are physically fit enough to endure an outback ordeal.
- If you're on any special medication, take extra supplies with you.
- Allow more time to get from point A to B in the outback than you would on the bitumen – a 50-km trek that might take less than an hour on tarred roads could take a day or more in the bush!
- Learn basic bush-survival techniques.
- Complete a basic mechanical course.
- Complete a basic first-aid course, and carry a first-aid kit.
- Carry a tool box, and know how to use it.
- Take a 4WD-training course and carry appropriate recovery gear.
- Take out appropriate travel and/or health insurance.
- Don't camp in riverbeds – they can flood unexpectedly.
- In tropical areas, don't swim, paddle, or fish unless you are 100 per cent sure that the water is crocodile-free.
- Drink plenty of water as you travel and supplement it with Aqualyte or some other rehydrant.
- Don't travel at night when wildlife or livestock may be on the roads.
- Finding that perfect shady spot and parking under a large tree is tempting, but beware of large branches which could drop and injure you or damage your vehicle, camper, or tent.
- Obtain relevant approvals in advance if you plan to visit or traverse farms, stations, or Aboriginal reserves.

- Don't take alcohol in or near Aboriginal communities designated as dry communities.
- Don't take photos of indigenous people without their permission.
- Leave gates as you found them – if they are open, leave them that way.
- Move aside for road trains.
- In tropical areas, avoid driving in the wet season – roads can become impassable within hours, and you could be stuck there for days!
- Don't enter roads or attempt water crossings that have been closed by officials.
- Keep calm if things go wrong.
- And finally, if you do get stranded or have a breakdown or other emergency, call for help, and stay with your vehicle until assistance arrives. *Do not leave your vehicle!*

28

Checklist for Award-Winning Tour Guides

After reading about the numerous tasks and responsibilities of an award-winning tour guide, here's a checklist that puts it all together:

- Be aware of your duty of care – you are responsible for your clients' safety and welfare.
- Know and plan your route.
- Identify possible risks on your tour.
- Know how to deal with an emergency.
- Always be courteous and polite.
- Your clients pay your wages – treat them with consideration and respect.
- Know your facts when giving your narrative – do your research; don't wing it or make things up. Take reference books with you for back-up
- Prepare your presentation in advance, then practice, practice, practice!
- Make your narrative compelling and entertaining – *it's show time, folks!*
- Learn how to project your voice.

- Position yourself for best effect when delivering your presentation or commentary.
- Be enthusiastic and passionate about your subject.
- Modify your tour and presentation for groups with special interests or special needs.
- Speak slowly and clearly.
- Don't be sarcastic or use slang.
- Wear a watch, be punctual, stick to your timetable.
- Do regular headcounts.
- Check the details: Have all the bookings been made? Are clients on the right tour? Does anyone have allergies or medical conditions you should know about? And so on.
- Check the weather before starting your tour.
- Think before you speak.
- Don't swear.
- Dress appropriately – look the part, and carry the right equipment for your particular tour.
- Be flexible and able to improvise – always have a Plan B.
- When faced with problems, be cool, calm, and in control.
- When implementing a solution to a problem, do so decisively.
- Keep things in perspective.
- Don't give groups options – they'll never all agree to one! You as the tour guide must make a decision and stick to it.
- Mix with everyone – no favourites.
- Don't be a sleaze or a sex machine.
- Don't be condescending or patronising.
- Be observant and intuitive – a SNAG (sensitive new-age guide!).
- Take an interest in current affairs – in your own country and around the world.
- Keep your problems to yourself – clients have paid to have a good time, not to listen to your sob stories!
- Deal with confrontation if it's inevitable, but be reasonable – be assertive but not aggressive.
- Know your company's policies on a range of issues.
- Don't make promises on behalf of your employer.

- It may be your 100th trip, but the first for your customers – maintain your enthusiasm!
- Look after your own health and well-being.
- Be organised.
- Be confident but not cocky.
- Lead by example.
- Keep your first-aid knowledge current.
- Never stop learning about topics relevant to your tour.
- Develop a good rapport with others in the industry – tour operators, managers of venues, relevant government departments, park rangers, other guides, etc.
- Distribute customer-feedback forms at the end of a tour, and learn from them.
- Keep up with the paperwork.
- Aim to give your clients the best visitor experience of their lives – every time!
- Remember that you play a valuable role in the tourism industry.
- Be proud of your profession – you are special and highly skilled!

Now turn back to Chapter 5. You may want to modify the initial list you made of what it takes to be an award-winning tour guide – we guarantee your second list will be longer than the first!

Desirable Skills and Knowledge   **Desirable Character Traits**

_____   _____

_____   _____

_____   _____

_____   _____

_____   _____

_____   _____

_____   _____

_____   _____

After twenty-one days of challenging remote-area travel, clients on a Global Gypsies tag-along tour celebrate completing the 2,000-km Canning Stock Route, known as the Loneliest 4WD Track in the World. (Photo courtesy Global Gypsies)

29

Recommended Memberships, Networking Opportunities and Courses

Joining tourism-related industry organisations and relevant associations and creating a network for yourself or your company isn't mandatory in order to become an award-winning tour guide. However, it certainly helps establish you as a valued and contributing member of the industry, builds your credibility and reputation, teaches you a lot of new things, and creates a framework of colleagues, supporters, and allies.

In Australia, consider the following initiatives; similar opportunities will exist where you live:

- Join the Guiding Organisation of Australia and your local or regional Tour Guides Association.
- Attend relevant presentations, forums, seminars, and workshops.
- Become an honorary ranger with the Department of Parks and Wildlife (or similar organisation in your state).
- Volunteer to sit on relevant boards, councils, or committees, and be an enthusiastic participant. Over the years, we've been involved with the Tourism Council of WA Board, Nature Based Tourism Advisory Board, Tourism Industry Reference Group, Tour Guides

WA, Honorary Ranger Program of Department of Parks and Wildlife, Forum Advocating Cultural and Ecotourism, Motor Trade Association 4WD Industry Committee, Tourism Industry Advisory Council, Desert Knowledge Cooperative Research Centre, and the Caravan Industry Association. If you don't have the time or inclination to sit on boards or committees, at least join relevant organisations and attend their meetings and events.

- Sign up for relevant e-newsletters issued by tourism-related organisations.
- Go on tours run by operators in your area to improve your knowledge and experience (you will probably need to pay, but they may give you an industry discount).
- If possible and relevant, obtain Eco-Tour Guide accreditation through Ecotourism Australia or your local organisation (you need practical experience for this, although not necessarily a degree, so it may be something you aim to do once you've been guiding for a while).
- Join outdoor, bushwalking, caving, canoeing, star-gazing, conservation, or whatever-interests-you clubs – you'll gain experience and knowledge, have a great time, meet some new friends, and make some valuable contacts.
- Try to get some practical experience as a volunteer or assistant guide.

Recommended Courses

Ongoing education, whether part-time or full-time, is a great way to reach the top and stay on top as a tour guide. Here are some suggestions on courses to take:

- If you're still at secondary school, participate in vocational programs (where available); then when you finish school:
- Take practical, recreational courses in such subjects as four-wheel driving, first-aid, bush craft and/or survival skills, flora, fauna, astronomy, or whatever takes your fancy.

- If you'd like to do some instructing in four-wheel driving or other outdoor activities, get a Certificate IV in Workplace Training and Assessment, and then specialise in your preferred subject.

- Attend a hands-on *non-accredited* commercial tour-guide training course such as the one developed by Global Gypsies (http://www.globalgypsies.com.au). Other organisations in Australia such as Savannah Guides also offer quality commercial courses (http://savannah-guides.com.au/about/savannah-guide-schools/).

- Take a part-time or full-time *accredited* tourism-related course at TAFE or other registered training organisation (RTO) near you. There are too many colleges and RTOs offering tourism-related courses to list here, but an Internet search should help you find a provider close to home.

- Accredited courses to consider could include an entry level Certificate I in Australian Indigenous Culture or Certificate II in Tourism or such trade level courses as a Certificate III in Tourism, Certificate III in Guiding, Certificate IV in Travel and Tourism, or Certificate IV in Guiding. (Course descriptions are correct at the time of writing but are subject to change.)

- Accredited courses are made up of various components or 'units'. At some institutions, it may be possible to take one or more of these units rather than take a complete course. For example, units relevant to tour guiding include Work as a Guide, Provide Arrival and Departure Assistance, Coordinate and Operate a Tour and Lead Tour Groups. If this is your preference, check with the provider to see if taking individual units can be arranged. If so, find out whether you could earn an accreditation for that single unit or if participation would be purely for your personal self-development.

- If nothing suitable is available locally, then doing a course online with a recognised learning institution could be an option. Online tourism-related courses with various commercial non-RTO organisations are also available, but do some investigation before you sign up to make sure they're legit and that they'll be teaching you what you want to learn!

- If you're keen to pursue even more advanced-level courses and earn a degree in tourism and/or travel covering the broader managerial, administrative, marketing, hospitality, and commercial aspects of the industry, check out the institutions below and the courses they offer. (The list is taken from the Australian Education Network web site and is correct at the time of writing, but do your own research to see what is currently available.)

Undergraduate Tourism Courses On Campuses in Australia	
Blue Mountains International Hotel Management School	Bond University
Central Queensland University	Charles Sturt University
Edith Cowan University	Flinders University
La Trobe University	Murdoch University
Southern Cross University	Swinburne University of Technology
Think Education Group	University of Canberra
University of South Australia	University of Tasmania
University of Technology, Sydney	University of Western Sydney
Victoria University	
Postgraduate Tourism Courses On Campuses in Australia	
Bond University	Flinders University
La Trobe University	Murdoch University
Raffles College of Design and Commerce	Southern Cross University
The University of Notre Dame Australia	The University of Queensland
University of South Australia	University of Tasmania
University of Technology, Sydney	Victoria University

Our last bit of advice on this subject is:

Remember that training and technical abilities are not enough!
You also need personality, people skills, and passion!

Tour Guide Tale #9: Dealing with Groupies

Some people think that one of the perks of being a tour guide is that you become absolutely irresistible to your clients and attract groupies. Is it true?

Just like any profession that puts you in a leadership role, be it teacher, politician, company boss, or tour leader, you can definitely become a chick magnet or guy magnet, particularly on an extended tour when everyone is far from home. As a professional guide, how should you handle this kind of attention?

If you're single and you're interested in the person, you may want to follow things up *after* the tour – but not during it, please! You'll stuff up the synergy of the tour, make things awkward for all the clients (yes, of course they'll all find out, usually within hours!), create problems for you and the person involved, lose the group's respect, and just generally make a mess of things. So don't fool around while the tour's in progress! It's up to you what happens once the tour is finished.

But what if you're *not* interested? If the attention is unwanted and unwarranted? How do you let the client down gently? This has happened to Jeremy on several occasions. Initially, he tries to avoid the problem by wearing a wedding ring and speaking about Jan frequently.

But if the client doesn't take the hint and keeps on flirting, he has a private chat with the infatuated groupie, explaining that he's flattered by the attention but is in a committed relationship and so he's really not interested in taking things to another level. That usually does the trick.

However, on one occasion, a gorgeous and very besotted young European woman just refused to get the message. Even after the tour was over, she kept phoning him, trying to arrange a private catch-up. So Jeremy invited her home for coffee, with Jan playing the happy housewife.

They were both extremely warm and welcoming to their visitor, and Jeremy was (as the Aussies say) all over Jan like a rash – he'd never been so affectionate! But it worked. After the disappointed love-struck lady left our home, he never heard from her again. She was a nice person, and hopefully, she'd been let down in a way that spared her feelings and dignity as much as possible.

Hopefully, she still retained fond memories of her Australian holiday even though she didn't end up living happily ever after with the tour guide as happens in the movies.

30

Recommended Reading
and Reference Material

Whether you get your information from books, magazines, articles, scientific papers, or the Internet, you need to have plenty of it in order to become an award-winning tour guide.

Here's a list of reference material we find useful – you can probably source similar material where you live. If not, try purchasing it online; second-hand copies may also be available on such web sites as eBay or Gumtree.

When using phone apps, remember to download them *before* you leave home, when you have reception and a fully charged phone!

Astronomy: Star Chart; SkyScout; free and/or paid iPhone apps.

Birds: Simpson and Day Field Guide (plastic cover); free and paid i-phone apps (some have photos and bird calls)

Conditions: WA Department of Parks and Wildlife Services issues regular updates on road, bushfire, and other conditions in national parks (a similar authority in your area may do the same); Department of Main Roads or local Shires can provide updates on road conditions in urban, regional, and remote areas; free and paid apps on iPhones.

Culture: Aboriginal Australia and Torres Strait Islands and Outback Australia books (both from the *Lonely Planet* series); *Traveller's Guide to Aboriginal Australia*; miscellaneous legends and history and cultural books; *First Footprints* TV series.

Fauna: Bush books and *Discovery Books* series (pocket-sized books by WA Department of Parks and Wildlife); *Venomous Creatures of Australia* (international clients *love* reading about scary critters!); various Green Guides and wildlife books; free and paid iPhone apps – too many to list here!

Flora: Wildflowers of the Western State; Guide to Wildflowers of Southwestern Australia; *Guide to Wildflowers of Western and Central Australia*; free and paid iPhone apps

First-Aid: St John's Ambulance publishes a number of books and online information.

Food: Various bush food books (there's even a bush tucker bookshop!); outback cooking books; camp oven cookbooks by our friend Jo Clews; and others.

General: ABC bookshops have a great range of nature books and DVDs – and don't forget David Attenborough's wonderful programs!

Language: Various phrasebooks (depending on your audience); also Jibbigo, Translate, and other free and paid iPhone apps.

Maps: Google online maps; electronic HEMA and/or GPS RAC maps; and good old-fashioned hard-copy maps!

Public speaking: Range of books available from the library or online; or join Rostrum or other organisations where you can practice your public-speaking skills.

Weather: Various weather books and web sites (we like the Bureau of Meteorology's four-day weather forecast); some motoring organisations offer free text weather-alert services; numerous free and paid iPhone apps.

More in-Depth Reading

If you're keen to read about tour guiding in more depth, here are some other reference books you may find useful:

- *Tour Guiding Research: Insights, Issues and Implications* by Betty Weiler and Rosemary Black

- *Handbook for Tour Guides* by Nimit Chowdhary

- *An Interpretive Approach to Tour Guiding: Enriching the Experience* by John Pastorelli

- *How to be a Tour Guide: The essential training manual for Tour Managers and Tour Guides* by Nick Manning

31

Career Opportunities

(Please note that the opinions in this chapter are based on available statistics and our own personal impressions, observations, and experiences. For detailed and current statistics and a more formal overview of workplace opportunities in your area, please consult Tourism Australia or your state government tourism office.)

In Australia generally, and possibly where you live, tourism is a major contributor to the economy. Employment opportunities exist in a range of tourism sectors including travel, accommodation, events, conventions, transport, attractions, restaurants, visitor services, and tour guiding.

According to Tourism Australia, which is the organisation responsible for marketing Australia as a destination, the tourism industry is experiencing continuous growth. In 2013 and 2014, Australia received 6.7 million international visitors (an 8.2 per cent increase over the previous year), while combined international and domestic tourism generated AUD$91 billion. Tourism was a major source of employment providing direct and indirect jobs for almost a million people or about four per cent of the country's population.

The majority of inbound tourists (those coming into Australia) visit the 'big-three destinations' – Sydney, Melbourne, and Queensland (Great Barrier Reef and the Gold Coast); stretch it to the 'big four', and they'll possibly get as far as Uluru (Ayers Rock) smack in the middle of the country or possibly Kakadu National Park in the far north.

Areas further west get a fairly small percentage of visitors with the exception of the Kimberley region in North West Australia and the Margaret River region in southwest WA with its reputation for fine wine.

Even though Western Australia (WA) may not get as many visitors as other parts of the country (about 800,000 international visitors or 13 per cent), tourism is one of the state's fastest growing industries.

According to Tourism WA and the peak industry body, the Tourism Council of WA, the state earns about AUD$8.3 billion from international, interstate, and intrastate tourists and more than 94,000 people, or 7 per cent of the state's population, are employed in the tourism industry. In regional WA, tourism is *the* largest employer, having just recently surpassed the mining and resources sector.

In 2014 and 2015, international tourists boosted Perth businesses by more than AUD $133 million. Visitors from Malaysia and Singapore led the charge on the back of a low Aussie dollar while cruise-ship arrivals, new budget airlines, and tourists from the USA also increased. Unfortunately, nobody can tell us how many of these visitors actually took guided tours!

But even without this knowledge, the future for tourism in WA looks pretty bright. Some sources even predict that tourism could become WA's key export in the next fifteen years! It's certainly possible; we're right on Asia's doorstep. And in China alone, the middle class has grown from 500 million to 3.2 billion in the last few years – that's a lot of potential tourists!

Visiting cruise ships create job opportunities for local tour guides who take passengers on day trips to nearby attractions. (Photo courtesy Tourism Western Australia/Sun Princess.)

What Do These Numbers Mean to You?

Before you start rubbing your hands together with glee over these numbers and counting the income from all the tours you're going to be running, analyse the stats carefully and look at the bigger picture. And please keep in mind that we aren't trying to be negative with the following thought-starters, just realistic.

When considering the 6.7-million international arrivals to Australia, it's likely that some of those visitors may be coming here on business and may not have the time or inclination to go on a tour.

Another significant category included in the arrivals figures is that of Visiting Friends and Relatives (VFR). These folks will often stay in a suburban family home rather than a hotel and will have Uncle Bill or Aunt Betty as a volunteer tour guide driving them around in a private car. While the VFR group *does* spend a lot of money while they're here, we're not sure how much of it goes on commercial tours led by professional tour guides – we would guess it would be a fairly low proportion.

A significant number of our international visitors are currently coming from China and other parts of Asia. This is a market with very specific touring preferences which you'll need to learn about and provide for in very particular ways if you're planning to tap into it. If Chinese visitors are your target audience, you need to find out more about this very important market before you hang up your shingle. Check out http:// marketingtochina.com/top-10-things-know-chinese-tourists/ for some good tips. You should also attend China-Ready Workshops which are held by Tourism WA or possibly the tourism organisation in your area.

With regard to domestic (intrastate and interstate) tourists, it's always been a struggle for tour operators to convince Australians to holiday at home rather than spread their wings overseas. In 2013 and 2014, with a high AUD, the growth rate for Aussies taking overseas holidays was *four times higher* than that of Aussies taking domestic holidays. However, with the recent drop in the Aussie dollar, this trend could change, and we may see more Australians exploring their own backyard.

Global political unrest and the unpredictable activity of terrorists may also make the holiday-at-home option more attractive to Aussies. But a word of warning here – just be aware that, in our experience, many of those holidaying at home tend to prefer to do their own thing rather than join a commercial guided tour.

Another point to consider is, what if the preference to holiday at home also takes root overseas? At present, thousands of Europeans flock to Australia each year, hire a vehicle, and go exploring on their own. But even with attractive exchange rates and our reputation as a safe destination, it's possible that many of these tourists may decide to take holidays in their own countries in years to come rather than go globe-trotting with its perceived risks.

The aging population has seen cruising become an ever-increasing market sector. If you live in a city with a large port that's visited by cruise ships (such as Perth, Fremantle, or Bunbury, for example), escorted day trips are in high demand when the ships come in, and some ships carry up to 3,000 passengers! This can be a good source of income for tour guides, but in order to work out how much you might earn, check out the frequency and duration of ship visits.

A tourism sector that is often overlooked is the burgeoning self-drive market (we'll include both overseas and domestic visitors in this category). In our experience, not many domestic or international self-drivers on camping-type holiday will choose to go on commercial guided tours. This may be because many 'explorers' believe they can do it all themselves with the aid of a GPS (unless the destination or tour cannot be accessed without a guide or a special form of transport) or perhaps because they're on a budget.

In our opinion, more likely, tour clients will be staying in hotels or cabins or will have pre-booked a tour package and then choose some additional options after they arrive. The decision whether or not to take a commercial tour for these individuals is probably based on a combination of budget, age, and attitude.

Then there are the caravanners who fall within the self-drive market but have characteristics of their own. The thousands of grey nomads on the roads are usually on a budget, so you can't count on lots of them going on commercial tours. When they do, they are usually very attentive and keen to hear what the tour guide has to say. Sightseeing cruises, special-interest tours, and city tours seem to have the most appeal to this audience. They are often advancing in years, so you'll need to consider fitness levels and creature comforts on your tour if you're planning to target this group.

Special-interest and segmented niche-market tours are also increasing in popularity – guided tours by motorcycle, bicycle, walking tours, or tours for 'foodies', wine buffs, movie lovers, wildflower enthusiasts, birders, or photographers, for example – but keep in mind that these tours have a specific theme which could limit the take-up rate.

Possible job opportunities for tour guides exist at such venues as museums, government buildings, theatres, and art galleries. (Photo courtesy Tourism Western Australia/Art Gallery of WA.)

What's Happening in Your Area?

When considering job prospects in your area, think about how our broad-brush tourism observations apply to your particular situation. Consider your geographic location, the number of international, interstate, and intrastate tourists that visit, the amount and type of tourism experiences available to them, and the number of existing tour operators, venues, or attractions that employ tour guides.

To help you build a clearer picture of the tourism industry in your area and of the career opportunities which may exist, visit the local visitors centre, and pick up all the tour and attraction flyers you can. After you've studied them, select a few of the best-suited companies that interest you, study their web sites, go on one of their tours if possible so you know all about them, then ask for an appointment and go in for a chat.

Also speak to some 'tame' local tour operators and the Small Business Development Centre in your town or state. And if you want to start your own tourism business, draw up your own local industry profile and develop a SWOT analysis (we mentioned this before; it lists strengths, weaknesses, opportunities, and threats) and a business plan for your tourism idea – even if you only do it for your own benefit. It's worth the effort to help you understand the industry and identify the possible job opportunities before you dive in head first.

Your personal career opportunities will also depend on the type of tour guiding you want to do. If the kind of guiding and/or tours that you have in mind aren't available where you live, you might need to consider moving to a place where job prospects are more in line with what you want to do; there aren't many-desert trekking opportunities on Phillip Island, for example, or many snorkelling tours in Alice Springs! But whatever your tour-guiding goals, before you uproot your life and race off to follow your dream, do your homework first.

Many iconic tourist attractions, such as the Swan Bells in Perth, offer guided tours. Some venues employ paid guides; others use volunteers; and some prefer a combination of both. (Photo courtesy Tourism Western Australia/Swan Bells.)

Tour Guide Tale #10: Don't Let It Rain on Your Parade!

When running extended outback tours as we do, one of our biggest concerns is Mother Nature – maybe it will pour, maybe the roads will be closed or too muddy to traverse, or perhaps there will be a bushfire which makes it dangerous, or impossible, to follow our intended route. So we always need to have a Plan B and an alternative itinerary which we can implement on very short notice.

Our company terms and conditions give us the right to change the scheduled itinerary if we need to, and sometimes, we have no choice. One year, we had a wonderful five-day, self-drive, mini-outback 4WD and camping tour planned to a favourite outback destination in southeast WA called the Holland Track. We always try to choose the optimum time of year to run each trip. Normally, conditions for this tour would have been sunny and dry, but to our dismay, two days before departure, the heavens opened. The rain fell incessantly for forty-eight hours, and the track became impassable. The downpour was so heavy and so widespread that most other 4WD tracks in the southern half of the state were closed, too.

We had to decide whether to cancel the tour or design a different adventure – with *no* four-wheel driving - on very short notice! Thank goodness we had a contingency plan which we could put in place! The only problem then was to quickly book campgrounds and try to fill the days with activities other than 4WD fun!

Then we had to advise the clients who were, of course, very disappointed. But, hey! It's nature! What can you do? Some clients decided to take the Plan-B journey with us; some decided to pull out. By rights, we didn't need to refund any money to those who decided to cancel as the change in route was necessitated by inclement weather, but we did make partial refunds in several cases in order to preserve good customer relations.

Because we are a small company, we can make these types of decisions ourselves, but if you're employed by someone else, company policy may dictate 'no refunds'. As the tour guide on the spot, you'll be left to deal with any grumpy customers while trying to make the best of a bad situation and stay positive with the ones who've decided to stay on.

In these situations, the support from your office is invaluable as they'll be the ones making all the phone calls to find out road conditions, book alternative group accommodation, handle refunds (if any), help you smooth ruffled feathers, and so on.

These types of situations also highlight the need for clients to take out private travel insurance – not just in case they have to cancel in advance for a medical or family emergency, but in case the trip can't go ahead as planned due to circumstances beyond the company's control.

Urge your clients to take out travel insurance – even for domestic tours – and encourage them to read the small print so they know what situations are covered.

Looking for Work

In WA, you can search for current employment opportunities on the web sites of the following organisations. Similar information should be available from relevant web sites catering for other geographical areas as well:

- JobsWA: http://www.jobs.wa.gov.au/
- Seek.com.au – http://www.seek.com.au/
- Department Training and Workforce Development – http://www.dtwd.wa.gov.au/
- Discover Your Career – http://discoveryourcareer.com.au/discover-tourism/
- Careers in Tourism in WA – http://www.tourism.wa.gov.au

- Workforce Development Centres – http://www.dtwd.wa.gov.au/employeesandstudents/workforcedevelopmentcentres/Pages/default.aspx

You should also:

- Keep an eye on the 'wanted' ads in the employment section of newspapers and in various tourism publications and e-newsletters.
- Visit your local visitor centre, obtain brochures of destinations and tour operators, and become familiar with what's available in your area.
- Prepare a good CV and send it out to tour operators who appeal to you with a killer cover letter (get help from friends if you need to – your first impression on a prospective employer is crucial!).
- Follow your CV up with a phone call. Don't be disappointed if nobody responds to your initial letter; some employers are just too busy, don't have the staff, or just don't have the professional courtesy to respond. And don't give up if you're not swamped with job offers in the first week. Just keep trying and follow up the companies that you're really keen to work with every few months.
- Offer to work as a trainee tour guide for a company or attraction to get some experience under your belt (even if it's not exactly what you want and the initial pay is lousy or non-existent).
- Start your own business – a tough road to choose with lots of obstacles but also lots of rewards if you succeed. We'll cover this in the next chapter.

What Kind of People Become Tour Guides?

Tour Guides come from a variety of backgrounds – farmers, academics, business people, mechanics, builders, teachers, engineers, bus drivers, truck drivers, you name it. But as a rule, they are people who want to do something a little out of the ordinary, they don't want a normal nine-to-five desk job, they like being their own boss, and they enjoy working outdoors. People just like *you*!

Graduates of a Global Gypsies' hands-on, two-day tour-guide training course in their bush classroom. (Photo courtesy Global Gypsies.)

What Are the Job Prospects?

This is a tough one to answer because the tourism picture varies from place to place and can vary from year to year. From a tour guide's perspective, each destination offers totally different visitor experiences, types of tours, and job opportunities and attracts different target audiences. At one time, the Gold Coast might be booming; at another time, perhaps the Kimberley, Kakadu, or Tasmania might be the flavour of the month.

Tourism can be impacted by so many factors – global, national, and local events, the exchange rate of the Aussie dollar, consumer confidence, travel trends (think of the current popularity of 'foody' tourism, walking tours, cultural tours, 'voluntourism' and cruises, for example), demographics of travellers (i.e., huge wave of baby boomers), natural disasters like cyclones or tsunamis, cost of airfares, and so on. The volume of tourists can also be affected by school holidays, wildflower season, animal behaviour, and more.

Unfortunately, in tough financial times, tourism and hospitality often feel the pinch first. But like most things, tourism goes in cycles. It's really a case of keeping up with current affairs and consumer trends while continuously gazing into a crystal ball. The only things that really stay the same for a tour guide are the basic generic guiding principles that we've outlined in this book!

Because of weather conditions, guiding work can be seasonal, so you may only be able to earn an income for part of the year. Think of the outback where travelling is too hot in the summer months; the Kimberley where there are torrential summer rains and tropical cyclones during 'the wet', when roads have to close; or beach resorts where it's a bit too cold in the winter for most people to swim. You'll either need to squirrel away your finances in the busy times or figure out how you'll earn money in the off season.

Salary-wise, in WA, a tour guide can expect to earn somewhere around AUD $250–$300 per working day, more if you're lucky. If you want to get rich, tour guiding is not the best way to do it. But if you can live on the income, we think it's a wonderful career that has lots of other rewards.

There are also a number of volunteer guiding opportunities out there. If you're retired, or for whatever reason don't want or need a pay cheque, look for a position in which you can give your time freely doing what you love. This will enable you to share your knowledge and indulge in your passion for flora, fauna, heritage, art, architecture, culture, science, or whatever else takes your fancy, or you could give tourists a warm welcome when they arrive at the airport.

While on that subject, the issue of paid vs volunteer guides is a frequent topic of conversation in the industry, and there are varying points of view on how volunteer guiding impacts on the job prospects of those who are trying to earn a living from it. We believe that unpaid and/or volunteer guiding does have an impact on the potential employment opportunities for paid guides.

However, from an industry perspective, volunteers are a huge plus as they provide a valuable service to tourists. Without them, it's possible there might be no guides in those positions due to financial constraints. So, yes, volunteers compete with paid guides in some respects, but the two actually complement each other.

Technology

Another interesting factor with possible long-term ramifications for the tour-guiding profession is technology. Many jobs are threatened or being made redundant by new technology, and tour guiding is no different. How often do you see tourists walking around museums, art galleries, parks, or cities wearing headphones and listening to pre-recorded sightseeing information?

What about Google Glass, virtual tours, and no doubt other emerging technologies which alleviate the need for a human guide altogether? These are interesting challenges and ones that we as tour guides can only overcome by being so absolutely brilliant, enthusiastic, and warm and by making the visitor experience so overwhelmingly personalised that technology can't replace us! Be an award-winning tour guide! Ensure that your clients enjoy a top-quality experience every single time and get value for their money!

You can also turn the situation to your advantage and put technology to work for you – there are numerous phone apps that are now available that can help you do your job even better.

Job Opportunities

In WA alone, there are over 400 accredited tour companies offering an excellent product who could be potential employers! If you'd like to work with them (or at least get an interview), then get your CV and killer letter together and make an approach. In addition to Perth and Fremantle, there's plenty to see and do in such regional destinations as Albany, Broome, Bunbury, Esperance, Kalgoorlie, Kununurra, Margaret River, Pemberton, Walpole, and more, so consider applying to companies in these areas as well.

A list of accredited tour operators in WA (and throughout Australia) is available at http://trustthetick.com.au/. A number of these operators have also been honoured with tourism awards. In WA, these include:

- Adams Pinnacle Tours
- Adventure Wild
- Alek and Gina's Ningaloo Ecology Cruises Glass Bottom Boat Exmouth
- APT Kimberley Wilderness Adventures
- Aussie Wanderer

- Aviair
- Brian Lee Hunters Creek Tagalong Tours
- Bungoolee Tours
- Country Escapes in WA Tours
- Donnelly River Cruises
- Geraldton Air Charter
- Global Gypsies Tours and Training
- Kimberley Wild Expeditions
- Kingfisher Tours
- Koomal Dreaming
- Mills Charters
- Ningaloo Safari Tours
- Rockingham Wild Encounters – Penguin Island Ferry and Cruises
- Rottnest Fast Ferries
- Sail Ningaloo
- Segway Tours WA
- Skydive Jurien Bay
- Southern Skydivers
- Tagalong Tours Broome
- Taste Bud Tours
- Three Islands Whale Shark Dive
- Top Drop Tours
- Triple J Tours
- Two Feet & a Heartbeat – Guided Walking Tours
- Uptuyu Aboriginal Adventures
- Urban Indigenous
- Wagoe Beach (Kalbarri) Quad Bike Tours
- Wilderness Getaways

Job opportunities may also exist at such venues as:

- AQWA (state aquarium)
- Art galleries (government and commercial)
- Fremantle Prison

- Government House
- Kings Park
- Museums
- National Parks (camp hosts or park rangers)
- Parliament House
- Perth Mint
- Perth Zoo
- Rottnest Island
- Scitech
- Swan Bells
- Wineries
- Wildlife parks, and numerous other destinations.

There are also several large overseas or interstate-owned companies that run a variety of tours in WA that may have guiding opportunities available.

Some companies prefer to use guides with specialist knowledge in such fields as flora, fauna, ornithology, biology, marine science, astronomy, or history; others hire multi-lingual guides or those with indigenous or cultural expertise, while still others prefer all-rounders.

List Yourself on the Web

A number of overseas-based web sites list and recommend *individual tour guides* by region. These sites can be helpful for solo operators and are particularly useful to generate business in quiet times. Consider registering yourself and/or your tours on:

http://tourguides.viator.com
www.toursbylocals.com
www.yourtouristguides.com

There are also numerous web sites that promote tours generally – too many to list them all here! Type 'tours' into Google, and take your choice of which ones you'd like to try, checking out the free ones first. But for starters, get your tours listed on the Tourism Australia and your local state tourism authority web sites. Then try Trip Advisor and such other sites as:

http://www.truelocal.com.au
http://triptide.com.au/
https://www.responsibletravel.com

Tour Guide Tale #11: Put Prudence Before Profit!

In 1999, eighteen people, many of them from Australia and New Zealand, were killed in a canyoning accident in Interlaken, Switzerland. Authorities issued weather reports to local tour operators, warning them of possible rainstorms and snow thaws. Such conditions were common in the area and known to cause life-threatening flash floods in the downstream canyons.

The tour companies and their guides could have cancelled their abseiling and canyoning tours on this day. Some did, but several ignored the warnings and continued to operate their tours as scheduled. Horrifically, and as predicted, flash floods suddenly rushed into the canyons. Several tour guides and their clients were trapped in the narrow canyons and drowned.

Making the decision to continue operating the tours in potentially life-threatening conditions – possibly for economic reasons – appears to have resulted in a catastrophe. With better judgment and by putting prudence before profit, this disaster may have been avoided.

The moral of the story? Show good judgment, and check the weather reports. If in doubt, pull out!

32

Want to Start Your Own
Tour Business?

We've seen so many enthusiastic, talented people with new ideas who have invested their life savings to start an exciting new tourism business. Sadly, we see too many of them a few years later with shattered dreams – their idea didn't work, they've left the industry, and now they're disappointed and strapped for cash. We don't want you to be one of them.

We're going to share our tips that we've learnt from the School of Hard Knocks to help you avoid some of these pitfalls. But first, we'd like to tell you how and why we started our business and how we've always managed to run it on a shoestring.

How We Started Our Business

We started Global Gypsies in Perth, Western Australia, in 1997. Our primary product then was escorted, self-drive, 4WD tag-along tours into the Australian outback in which clients drive their own or hired 4×4 vehicles and travel in a small convoy led by an expert guide.

Since then, we've expanded our product range to include such innovative new products as:

- Dog-along tours: for clients who won't travel without their best friends; we design special itineraries which incorporate attractive settings but exclude national parks (which don't allow pets).
- Caravan safaris: same concept as a 4WD tag-along but for caravans and camper trailers; we design softer itineraries and stay on the bitumen.
- Science safaris: voluntours in which clients work with scientists and researchers from the WA Department of Parks and Wildlife on hands-on projects to protect and preserve endangered species of flora and fauna.
- Dust to Dust: a unique service which enables clients to have their ashes scattered in the outback.

Once or twice a year, we also escort tours to such exotic overseas destinations as the Great Silk Road, Africa, India, North and South America, Antarctica, and other faraway places.

Meanwhile, with the help of expert instructors, our training division delivers courses in tour guiding, outback skills, four-wheel driving, and caravan towing. Some of these expansion and diversification initiatives were financially driven; others evolved because we saw a window of opportunity.

About the Authors

*Jeremy Perks and Jan Barrie, tour operators, trainers, authors, travellers,
and founders of Global Gypsies. (Photo courtesy Global Gypsies.)*

Jeremy is the tour guide in the company; he's also the itinerary planner,
senior instructor, and operations manager. He's a natural leader, excellent
bushman, and great communicator.

Born in South Africa, Jeremy immigrated to Australia in 1996. In his
youth, he was a teacher, an officer in South Africa's elite armed forces,
and a qualified mechanic. He also helped establish and manage a highly
successful advertising agency with over 500 staff in Johannesburg. He
later opened a branch office of the agency in Kenya but then turned his
back on corporate life.

He sold his shares and went to run a safari camp near Lake Naivasha in Kenya's magnificent Rift Valley – if you've seen a photograph of pink flamingos in Africa, it was probably taken near there.

Not everyone aspiring to be a tour guide has, or needs, this kind of eclectic background, but Jeremy's natural aptitude combined with his life experiences have given him all the special skills required to become an award-winning guide. A jack of all trades and master of many, Jeremy tried lots of jobs, but none of them felt quite right until he discovered tour guiding in his late 30s. Perhaps this strikes a resonant chord with you!

Jan is responsible for the administration and marketing side of the company. Born in the UK, she immigrated to the USA with her parents where she studied journalism and later worked in a series of jobs including hospitality, sales, and public relations.

Then came a decade of solo travels through Europe and Australia. After living in Melbourne and working on Queensland's Great Barrier Reef, she settled in Perth, Western Australia, one of the most remote and beautiful capital cities in the world. For several years, she was a public relations manager, but then the travel bug hit again. In the early 90s, she went to live and work in Kenya where she was employed by a large advertising agency and became the travel writer for the country's daily newspaper.

Then fate and Cupid stepped in when your authors met up in Nairobi. After a year together, they decided to quit their jobs and travel overland through Eastern and Southern Africa as a photojournalist team. Because they were contributing articles to several international newspapers and magazines, they were invited to stay at dozens of wonderful safari camps, hotels, lodges and to experience such unforgettable activities as walking with elephants, communing with gorillas, transporting rhinos by helicopter, and riding in hot-air balloons. They saw the best and the worst of the tourism industry from front-of-house to behind-the-scenes, met some incredible people, and had some exciting and frequently hair-raising experiences!

When the funds ran out and their idyllic on-the-road lifestyle was no longer sustainable, they decided to return to civilisation. Jeremy applied for Australian residency and when it was granted, they came to Perth. While travelling, they had often spoken of starting their own company, so within weeks of arriving in WA, Jan and Jeremy registered the Global Gypsies name and started planning their first tour.

Our Customer Base

Global Gypsies offers a niche-market product – escorted self-drive 4×4 tours to such remote-area destinations such as the Canning Stock Route, the Kimberley, Rudall River (Karlamilyi) National Park, Karijini National Park, the Great Central Road, Tracks of Len Beadell, the Holland Track, Great Australian Bight, and many more challenging areas inaccessible by two-wheel-drive vehicles.

Because participants need to undertake a fair amount of pre-trip planning and preparation in order to join these tours and because of the distance from Perth to pretty much anywhere, this puts a bias on West Australian residents as our potential clients.

On a Global Gypsies tag-along tour, clients drive through the outback in their own or hired 4×4 vehicles, travelling in a convoy led by an expert guide – independent, but not alone. (Photo courtesy Global Gypsies.)

These factors also minimise the number of customers we attract from the eastern states or overseas as does the cost of hiring a vehicle to join our convoys. The nature of the product also narrows our market down to intrepid souls with a pioneering spirit.

While we run a number of tours to different destinations each year, we usually don't repeat the same tour twice over a twelve-month period. Therefore, we don't get heaps of first-time customers doing the same tour each year, as you would if you were offering a weekly departure from Broome through the Kimberley, for example.

Instead, we get a lot of repeat customers who come back each year to take a *different* tour, plus new customers who eventually follow the same purchasing pattern. This means, we have to promote several different tours each year to a loyal customer base instead of just one tour to a bevy of new clients.

So how and where do we source our customers? Most Global Gypsies clients come from Western Australia (85 per cent), about 10 per cent from interstate, and about 5 per cent from overseas. We reach them through our web site, quarterly e-newsletters, articles in newspapers and magazines, stands at trade shows, and word-of-mouth recommendations.

Because we're a small family-run, home-based company with a niche-market product and relatively low turnover, we can't afford to advertise, particularly overseas (except through our web site).

Neither can we afford to pay commissions of up to 30 per cent to international wholesale agents (wholesalers) to promote and on-sell our products to retailers. Retailers, in turn, take part of that commission and on-sell our tours to their customers at a recommended retail price.

Plus, Western Australia is pretty far away from anywhere – Perth is almost 4,000 km from Sydney! So for all these reasons, it's logical that the local market represents the largest slice of the pie.

A company which offers regular departures, has online booking facilities, has a larger promotional budget, can handle larger customer capacity (known in the trade as 'bums on seats'), pays wholesaler commissions, and whose product has a broader customer appeal would probably have a larger percentage of international tourists in its client profile.

Surviving on a Shoestring

We've structured our business so that we have minimal overheads. As we've explained, clients need to own, or hire, a 4WD vehicle to join our tours, so we don't need to own a fleet of coaches, have a big garage or depot to store them in, or employ a large staff to drive them all.

The majority of our business is done via the Internet or on the phone, so we don't really need a traditional office; therefore, we run our business from home. It can get a bit crowded sometimes with three or four of us coming and going, and you have to be disciplined about your working hours, but having a home-based business works fine for us and saves us heaps of money.

Because we both have marketing backgrounds, we write and issue media releases ourselves and rely on print and electronic *editorial* for our publicity. Radio and TV advertising is way too expensive for us. We seldom pay for print advertisements, and when we do, we always try to get editorial coverage as well.

With the help of a professional webpage design and hosting company, we maintain a simple, relatively inexpensive web site which we try to keep interesting, up to date, and full of photos.

We treat our client database like gold and stay in touch with customers frequently – but not often enough to become annoying! We issue a quarterly e-newsletter which we write ourselves and keep light, newsy, and soft sell.

We maintain a Facebook page and Twitter and Instagram accounts – although we're still learning how to use the last two effectively! We limit ourselves to participating in two well- targeted local trade shows a year, and join relevant boards and committees to keep our fingers on the pulse, build our networks, and put something back into the industry.

We work hard on developing mutually beneficial relationships with suppliers, sponsors, and joint venture tour partners. We shop around for the best deals on office and operational equipment, telephone services, uniforms, and other essentials.

We employ an on-the-ball office manager and accountant to keep the finances in order, keep the taxman happy, and ensure that wages, superannuation, and bills are paid on time. That doesn't mean we relinquish responsibility for the finances – we would *never* do that, and if you start your own business, you mustn't either! It just means that we get someone else to do the data entries and the time-consuming drudge work that we aren't particularly good at and that would take us twice as long to complete. We always know how much we've got in the bank and keep a close eye on the figures. If you start your own business, you must do the same!

We started Global Gypsies with practically no money, which, in hindsight, we probably wouldn't recommend to other budding entrepreneurs. But again, because we have marketing backgrounds, are happy to live modestly (except for our passion for travel), have minimal capital outlays, and have no dependent children, we don't need a huge income. This is probably just as well because whenever we visit our accountant, he always tells us that we've made a 'lifestyle choice'!

We'd be the first to admit that the business model that we've created isn't a money-making formula, but it suits us. The freedom and independence our business provides keeps us, and our clients, from getting bored, allows us to constantly explore new destinations, gives us the flexibility to develop a range of tour themes (nature, art, science, history – whatever takes our fancy really!), and guarantees that we're bursting with enthusiasm on each trip.

But it may not be the right business model for you. Before you set up your new company:

1. Decide What You Want from the Business

Make no mistake, having your own tourism business is tough. Before you venture out on your own, decide what presses your buttons. Money? Lifestyle? Security? Independence? Think about how big you want your business to become; what you hope to achieve in five or ten years' time; what skills and aptitudes you're bringing to the business; what type of business model you want; and how much money you'll need to earn to cover expenses and make a profit (more on this topic later).

2. Decide on the Type of Tours You Want to Run

If you hope to run tours, do you want them to be coach tours, walking tours, tag-along tours, or something else altogether? What duration will they be – half-day, full-day, longer? What destinations do you want to visit? How often? What will your minimum/maximum numbers be? Will you always be the tour leader? Do you have a back-up guide in case you're ill or away or have to pull out of a tour halfway through? Do you need any other staff? Will the tours be catered? Will they be camping or accommodated? Is there a demand for the type of tour you want to run?

3. Do Your Research

Seek advice about the practical aspects of starting your business from your local, regional, and/or state tourism offices. They can provide you with a general introduction to the tourism industry and with business-planning tools to enable you to research and plan your own tourism business. They have research information and analyses about Australian tourism, including updates on consumer-travelling trends and insights into what's happening in the top tourism markets. You can use this research and analysis to help you make better-informed business decisions.

4. Get Some Industry Experience First

Consider working for another tour company to learn the ropes and get a feel for the industry before setting out on your own. We did that, and what we learned was invaluable, not just in learning what to do, but also in learning what not to do!

It's also helpful to take a short hands-on tour-guide training course like the one offered by Global Gypsies or Savannah Guides to find out what guiding is *really* like, or look for an equivalent course in your state. Alternatively, take the academic route and sign up for a tertiary or accredited course with a college or university (see Chapter 32 for suggestions).

5. Consider Your Finances

When establishing a company, the costs are considerable. Before you commit to your business:

- Take inventory of your finances, see how much you've got, and work out how much you'll need.
- Work out a budget/cash flow assuming you may have no income for two years.
- Work out your start-up costs for vehicle, equipment, office, staff, and launch costs. If you're buying a second-hand vehicle, be sure it is compliant with industry standards for operating tours.
- Calculate the overheads that you pay every month whether or not you run a tour – vehicle lease, phones, rent/mortgage, utilities, bank fees, and so on.
- Decide what wages you will pay yourself. Remember the old adage – 'If you're only working for wages, you have a job, not a business!'
- Include wages for a good bookkeeper and/or an accountant, office assistant, marketing person, and possibly other support staff (they could be permanent or part-time staff or

sub-contractors whom you employ as needed to provide the skills that you don't have!).

- Find out exactly what types of insurance you'll need and how much they will cost (public liability, vehicle, corporate travel, professional indemnity, employer's indemnity, etc.).

- Marketing can be expensive, particularly if you don't have a public relations or journalism background and have to rely on paid advertising. You'll also need to set up and maintain a good web site (more on these topics later). Don't expect tourism associations or visitor centres to do your marketing for you – this is a huge mistake made by many newcomers to the industry. Marketing your product or service on an ongoing basis will be up to *you*!

- What will your pricing structure be? How much will you need to charge for your product or service in order to cover tour costs, ongoing costs, wages, *and* make a profit? Will the price be affordable to prospective clients and represent good value for money?

- Investigate other sources of income such as training vouchers for courses from local business associations, government grants, rebates from the Australian Tourism Export Council, etc.

6. Be Aware of the Administration Involved

There's lots of red tape and administration involved with starting and running a business which can be time-consuming and frustrating.

- Find out what government regulations, accreditation, or licensing requirements you'll need to comply with and how much this will cost (registering your business name; licensing your vehicle; maintaining accreditation with the Department of Parks and Wildlife, Tourism Council, etc.).

- Consider who will be doing everything *other* than the guiding – looking after the accounts, taking bookings, processing payments, answering e-mails promptly, updating your web site, doing your marketing, and so on.

Some guides try to do it all themselves – the admin, marketing, finances, customer relations, the lot – plus run the tours! We don't know how they manage and certainly wouldn't recommend trying to tackle everything alone. Yes, you may be able to cope for a while, but you'll soon run yourself into the ground. It's unlikely you'll be able to do everything properly, and there certainly won't be any time left to enjoy your travels if that's why you set up your business in the first place.

Ideally, there should be one person in the field and one (or more) back in your office (or running a virtual office by remote control which is very possible with today's technology). So are you going to be the tour guide or the admin person? Our advice is to choose which hat you want to wear and share the load!

Share the load of running your tour business, or you won't have time to enjoy the benefits. (Photo courtesy Tourism Western Australia/Boranup Forest.)

7. Develop a Business Plan

Have clear objectives and write them down! The best way to do this is to draw up a business plan. When doing so, consider such factors as who your target market will be; what your strengths, weaknesses, opportunities, and threats are; and who your competition is.

Ask yourself all the questions we've posed previously such as *Is this business going to be viable and sustainable? Who is my target audience? How will I promote my business? What will my pricing structure be?* and so on. The Small Business Development Centre can help you develop a business plan; you can also download a generic template from http://www.business.gov.au.

The document that you produce doesn't have to be fancy, but going through the process of addressing all the questions is *invaluable* – it really focuses your thoughts and gives you a clear picture of where you are now, what resources you have, and the path you need to take to move forward.

8. Develop a Marketing Plan

It's not enough just to have a good business idea – build it, and they may *not* come! Here's a very important point; commit it to memory! *Without ongoing marketing and promotion, your business will fail.*

Marketing is an ongoing and costly expense, so hand-in-hand with your business plan, you need to develop a marketing plan. Again, you can download a generic template from http://www.business.gov.au. It's not as onerous as it sounds, and as with the business plan, going through the exercise will be extremely valuable.

If you're new to the marketing side of things:

- Consider who is going to do the marketing, how, when, from where, and if there's a cost involved for their time and expertise.

- Learn the difference between advertising and publicity – get your head around what's involved in both. Advertising is expensive, whereas you can generate publicity (almost!) for free if you know how to do it. To learn how to write a press release, visit https://www.ourcommunity.com.au/marketing/marketing_article.jsp?articleId=1575.
- Set a realistic marketing budget – get some general costs for paid promotion using TV, radio, newspapers, trade shows, etc.
- Get quotes for using a public-relations consultant to issue media releases to newspapers, magazines, or web sites, or write newsletters or a blog if you don't plan to do these jobs yourself.
- Get some quality stock photos and video clips relevant to your business, and issue them with your media releases or put them on your web site.
- E-marketing is now the main source of new business for a number of companies and also helps retain existing clients. You'll need to set up and maintain a professional-looking, mobile-friendly web site and update it regularly. This isn't a cheap exercise; you're looking at a *minimum* of about $20,000 to set it up and then ongoing maintenance and hosting costs after that.
- Consider how you'll drive clients to your web site and how much this will cost (we use publicity, e-newsletters, cross links, listing our business on travel portals, and paid Internet marketing tools such as Google AdWords and Facebook post boosts).
- Include costs (both time and money) of using social media such as Facebook, Instagram, Twitter, or other emerging platforms.
- Get quotes on producing printed brochures, flyers, business cards, and so on – even though the Internet is replacing much hard-copy material, you may still need something in print to distribute at trade shows, visitor centres, etc.
- Try to develop affiliations and partnerships with other tour companies involving cross-promotions and reciprocal web links to help raise awareness of your products and services and give you a broader marketing base.

- Word of mouth is by far the best way to promote your business. However, be aware that it takes many years of running successful tours before personal referrals from happy clients have a major impact on your bottom line. Consider word of mouth as a valuable supplement to your marketing efforts, not as the primary source of business.

9. Don't Give Up Your Day Job!

Have a financial cushion to tide you over for two or three years – it took us that long to get our first tours up and running with sufficient clients to make them viable. You may even have to run some tours at a loss initially so you don't get a bad reputation for cancelling trips. And remember that, during that time, you'll still have outgoing expenses whether or not you're bringing in any income.

It's best to keep a part-time job, as we both did, for the first few years. You'll work your behind off, but having a regular income will help keep your finances healthy until the business starts showing a profit. It will also reduce the stress you'll find yourself under. Until you become established, you'll continually wonder where the next dollar is coming from!

10. You Can't Live on Dreams

When we set up Global Gypsies many years ago, a lot of people said we were crazy. They told us it was a huge risk and that we'd have no job security. Maybe they were right then, but times have changed. Nowadays, even people in previously 'cushy' positions don't have guaranteed job security.

We, on the other hand, are masters of our own destiny and are our own bosses. Because our company is small, we can be creative, change direction quickly, diversify our products, and take advantage of trends and opportunities as they happen.

As it's turned out, even though the business hasn't made us rich and we've had to struggle through some tough times, we now have more job security and more job satisfaction than many of our former critics. We're independent, answerable to nobody but ourselves, and we love what we do.

Some folks say to us, 'You're living the dream!' But here's the rub. Your idyllic lifestyle needs to be combined with a healthy dose of practicality as well. You have to make enough money from your business to make ends meet and make a profit. You can't live on dreams.

Get Out There and Do It!

If after reading all our advice, following all our suggestions, and heeding all our warnings, you're still raring to go with your new business, then get out there and do it! Prepare yourself for long hours and lean times, but get it right, and you'll have the best job in the world!

Tour Guide Tale #12: Be a Life Changer!

We've met some wonderful people through our business, many of whom have become close friends – an unexpected bonus which we never anticipated when we started the company.

There is one couple in particular whose story we'd like to share; we'll call them Steve and Annie. In their 50s, they'd been office workers most of their lives, taking fairly traditional holidays to Bali or Europe. A devoted couple, they were keen anglers, boaters, car enthusiasts, and travellers but had always gone touring in a fairly 'tame' way, not feeling that comfortable or confident in outback situations.

They'd purchased a 4WD but had never run it through its paces or done much camping; most of their friends tended to prefer cruises and five-star hotels, and Steve and Annie didn't fancy 'going bush' on their own. Then they read an article about Global Gypsies and the company's 4WD training and self-drive tag-along tours in the travel pages of the local newspaper.

They signed up for a 4WD course, thoroughly enjoyed it, then booked a 4WD tour. Once they'd ventured into the outback with a guide, experienced sleeping under the stars, and learned how to handle the challenges of four-wheel driving in remote areas, they were hooked. They particularly loved the concept that when they went on a tag-along tour, they could explore places they'd never visit on their own and travel in the safety of a convoy led by an expert guide, independent but not alone.

They soon upgraded their vehicle, purchased a more comfortable tent, then later invested in an off-road camper trailer. They've been enjoying outback travel now for more than fifteen years.

Not only do they still come with us regularly on tag-along tours, but by travelling with us, they've also met a whole new group of friends with similar interests. They often go bush with them on their own adventures using the knowledge they've gained. Now that they're both retired, they spend much of their time on the road, exploring remote regions of our beautiful country and loving every minute of it.

As well as being valued clients, Steve and Annie have also become dear friends. They often tell us that going on our tours changed their lives. That always warms our hearts and makes us proud of what we do. Who could ask for a better reward?

33

Go for Gold!

Let's assume you've read this book from cover to cover, found a great guiding job, or started your own successful tour business. So what else do you need to do in order to become an *award-winning* tour guide?

Apart from following all the advice we've given you, there's one other tip. Blow your own trumpet! Generate some publicity for yourself and/or your tour! Enter tourism and/or business awards and go for gold!

Many local tourism industry associations such as the WA Forum Advocating Culture & Ecotourism (FACET) present an annual award for the best tour guide in the state. To apply, you have to make a lengthy submission. Yes, it's time consuming, and, yes, there's a lot of thinking, writing and time involved, but if you win, all your effort will be rewarded for many years to come. Also, it's a bit like doing a business or marketing plan – answering the questions really focuses your mind on what you're doing and keeps you on track.

If your state doesn't offer a tour-guiding award for individuals but does have other tourism award categories, you (or your employer) should put in a submission for a particular tour in the appropriate category.

There are also a number of business awards offered by Chambers of Commerce, newspapers, and other organisations. Enter them! You've got nothing to lose and everything to gain.

We'll never forget suggesting to some industry colleagues that they submit their tours for tourism awards. Their response left us gobsmacked. 'No way!' they said. 'What if we win? Then we'll have to live up to that high standard!' We see winning as an opportunity, not an obstacle, and you should, too.

In 2004, Jeremy won the FACET award for best individual tour guide in WA. In 2011, Global Gypsies won the Tourism Council of Western Australia Gold Medal for adventure tours and a Bronze Medal in Training for our tour-guide training course.

Apart from the kudos and feel-good factor generated by these wins, over ten years later, we still refer to these accolades in our marketing. Whether you are a finalist or take out a bronze, silver, or gold 'gong', winning awards gives you credibility, shows that you're serious about your company and your products, gets your name out in the marketplace, provides you with a competitive edge, gives your clients a warm fuzzy feeling, presents terrific publicity opportunities, and keeps you striving for excellence.

34

The End of the Tour

Like every good tour guide, we know when it's time to finish the tour. We've told you just about everything we can to help you become an award-winning guide, and we hope you've found the information of value.

To summarise, here again is our definition of what a tour guide is and does:

> *A tour guide is an enthusiastic, knowledgeable, responsible, passionate, multi-skilled interpreter delivering a consistently high-quality visitor experience.*
>
> *A tour guide's role is to equip clients with the skills and knowledge to appreciate, respect, understand, and interact with natural, cultural, historical, or built attractions.*

In a nutshell, here are the pros and cons of the job. We'll start with the negative aspects first so we can save the best till last!

Negatives of Tour Guiding

- It's not all glamour!
- It pays less than some other professions.
- You'll work long hours.
- It can involve hard physical work.
- You can suffer from customer overdose.
- You may be away from family and friends for long stretches.
- It can be hard on relationships – you need a very supportive and understanding partner.
- You're on call 24/7 – there are no weekends, public holidays, or bad hair days.
- You may get short notice for tours and little rest between them.
- Some tour companies have a lot to learn about employee relations, communication, and appreciation of what you do.

Positives of Tour Guiding

- You'll be doing something you love.
- You'll never stop learning – there's always something new to find out about your passion, whether it's flora, fauna, history, architecture, astronomy, culture, geology, or some other fascinating topic.
- You can share your favourite topics with an appreciative audience.
- You can be fairly independent.
- You can work outside rather than in an office.
- It's a happy job – clients go on tour to have a good time.
- It's a positive working environment – you get constant reinforcement and emotional rewards.
- You may get to travel in your home country or abroad.
- You'll meet great people and make long-term friendships.
- There's a great camaraderie on the road with other guides.
- You're providing a genuine, tangible service.

- Sometimes, you'll have the wonderful opportunity to give your clients life-changing experiences.
- You can do the job till you're old and grey – like us!

Tour guiding is a fantastic career for the right person. We love it, and it's right for us. But is it right for you? Hopefully, this book has helped you find the answer.

About the Authors

Jeremy Perks is co-founder and Director of Global Gypsies Tours & Training which was established in Perth, Western Australia in 1997. He is a professional tour guide and a recipient of the prestigious FACET Tour Guide of the Year Award. In addition to leading tours, he is an accredited trainer with a Certificate IV in Workplace Training & Assessment (TAE) who delivers training courses in tour guiding, four-wheel-driving and towing. Jeremy is a qualified mechanic, was formerly an officer in the South African Defence Force and was a founder and director of a major advertising agency in Africa until he left the corporate world to become a tour guide.

Jan Barrie is co-founder and General Manager of Global Gypsies Tours & Training. Born in the UK, she has travelled extensively and lived and worked in the USA, UK, Australia and Africa. She has held senior management positions in marketing and public relations and is a published travel writer. Jan left the corporate world to establish Global Gypsies where she is responsible for administration, marketing and customer liaison.

Index

Printed in Great Britain
by Amazon